Gift of the Wind

The Corpus Christi Bayfront

By
Bill and Marjorie K. Walraven

Javelina Press
Corpus Christi, Texas

The Corpus Christi Bayfront

Gift of the Wind

It had no name. It came slowly across the Florida Keys and the Gulf of Mexico. Wind speeds were about 112 miles an hour, not much for a major storm.

But it pushed a 14-foot wall of water in front of it like a giant bulldozer, creating a veritable tidal wave. There had been reports from ships at sea, but Corpus Christians paid little heed. Three years earlier they had weathered a storm with a minimum of damage.

Then, on September 14, 1919, it struck, crushing docks, houses, and buildings. North Beach was swept clean. Downtown was a wreck. As many as 600 died.

But they did not die in vain, for this ill wind brought a deep channel, a port, and a storm-protected bayfront. This modern city is a gift of that horrible wind.

George Gongora

Goldbeck

FIRST EDITION

© 1997 Bill and Marjorie K. Walraven
Published in the United States of America
by Javelina Press, P.O. Box 1479, Corpus Christi, TX 78403

Books by Bill Walraven:

Humor:

Real Texans Don't Drink Scotch in Their Dr Pepper

Walraven's World or Star (Boarder) and Other Wars

All I Know Is What's on TV

History:

Corpus Christi: History of a Texas Seaport

El Rincon: A History of Corpus Christi Beach

With Marjorie K. Walraven:

The Magnificent Barbarians: Little-Told Tales of the Texas Revolution

Library of Congress Catalog Card Number : 97-93251

Walraven, Bill, 1925-

[1st ed]

Gift of the Wind: The Corpus Christi Bayfront

Bill and Marjorie K. Walraven;

Cover design by John C. Davis Jr.

Cover photos: Shoreline-Esmeralda "Lala" Salazar, Del Mar College
Lexington/Columbus ship and Lighthouse-George Gongora

Includes index

ISBN 9646325-2-7 perfect bound: $16.95

1. Texas--History--Corpus Christi. 1838-1997.—Anecdotes

1. Walraven, Marjorie K. II

September 14—A Date To Remember

September 14, 1926, can be considered the birthday of the modern city of Corpus Christi. Probably the greatest celebration ever held here christened the Port of Corpus Christi, as it brought deepwater access to the Gulf of Mexico.

The entrance of the destroyer USS Borie, carrying dozens of local, state and national leaders under the Bascule Bridge, highlighted the ceremonies, which included parades, pageants, concerts, and many speeches.

It was seven years to the day after the Great Storm of 1919, which persuaded federal officials to recognize the need for a protected harbor and vote money for a channel.

Corpus Christi was no longer a fishing village competing with Aransas Pass and Rockport for supremacy of the Coastal Bend.

But it would be more than a dozen years before funds could be found to build a seawall to protect Downtown from storm damage. Ad valorem taxes from seven area counties would make this project possible. Discovery of vast fields of oil and natural gas in the area coincided with the opening of the port, attracting heavy industry along the new harbor that soon extended miles inland.

Agriculture boomed as farmers and ranchers found a ready outlet for cattle, grain and cotton. And Corpus Christi became one of the fastest growing cities in America.

Art Museum of South Texas

This view is not one of the works in the permanent collection of the Art Museum of South Texas, but it is a permanent attraction. It is an ever-changing scene as art patrons view ships passing in the nearby channel.

Reef dwellers like the one below add color and interest to the exhibits at the Texas State Aquarium.

The show's about to start! No creatures are hiding as an aquarium diver prepares to serve dinner.

Photos-Greater C.C. Business Alliance

The Seawall along the Bayfront was completed in 1941. Later preservationists would bemoan any intrusion along the Bayfront that could harm its "natural beauty."

While nature in one of its more violent moments had made it all possible, the beauty is actually man-made—and a considerable improvement over nature. The Seawall and a later beautification project replaced a smelly, unsightly shoreline with tree-lined boulevards, landscaping, marinas and a new future for citizens and tourists alike.

No one planned it that way, but a unique city was created. Corpus Christi has a distinct back yard, where heavy and light industries are largely segregated from residential and business areas, and the Bayfront, its beautiful front yard.

But as the city grew, the business district, formerly centered near the water, dispersed, leaving many storefronts vacant.

Revival began with developments along the Bayfront—hotels, banks, restaurants, and tourist attractions. Then came the cultural complex near the harbor, the Bayfront Arts and Sciences Park, the Texas State Aquarium, and later the Gateway Park and Federal Courts Building.

Just north of the ship channel, the aquarium has become one of the top tourist attractions in the state. Watching the antics of the playful otters is a popular attraction.

Another attraction is mealtime, when the sea creatures put on a feeding frenzy show in the Flower Gardens Coral Reef. An outdoor sanctuary for injured birds offers another feeding scene. Healthy pelicans quickly learned the feeding schedule of their injured cousins and began showing up to get their share.

The aquarium itself is a classroom of sea life to be found in area bays, the Gulf of Mexico, and the Caribbean Sea.

In the early 1990s the Corpus Christi Museum of Science & History was vastly upgraded. Exhibits of artifacts from ancient Spanish shipwrecks and replicas of Christopher Columbus's fleet added a new dimension to the Hispanic heritage of South Texas.

At the museum visitors can go from a diorama of Carancahua Indians to models of a refinery and a working oil well, while a hands-on playground gives children a chance to have fun while they learn.

Across Chaparral Street can be found one of

The past meets the future as a replica of Columbus's Nina tests its sail power against a more modern conveyance. On weekly cruises landlubbers can learn the ropes.

A *Mirador*—lookout—on the Seawall frames the cruising shrimp boat *Sharkey*.

the most extensive collections of Japanese and Oriental art in the country. The Asian Cultures Museum and Educational Center collection is so extensive only a small portion of it can be displayed at one time. This allows the museum to rotate exhibits so that five complete shows can be presented without showing any item twice. Probably the most impressive collection held by this unique educational facility is a collection of 200 paintings of Japanese emperors dating back to ancient times.

The new facility includes classrooms for teaching languages and cooking. Mrs. Billie Trimble

World War II sailors from Corpus Christi Naval Air Station spend their liberty feeding seagulls on the seawall. This period gave the city its reputation as a good Navy town.

A pilot's-eye view of the aircraft carrier *Lexington* at its permanent berth on Corpus Christi Beach. Up close it's a big ship. A pilot landing on the open sea sees it as a small boat.

Soldiers train on North Beach during World War I. Rifle and machine gun firing ranges were located in the salt flats.

McGregor Collection-C.C. Museum

C.C. Public Library

Cruz/Galveston: Courtesy of USS Lexington Museum

Chandler founded the museum in the 1960s to build a "bridge" between Asian countries and the United States, specifically Corpus Christi.

Centerpiece of the cultural complex is the Watergarden, which connects the Museum of Science & History with Harbor Playhouse, the Art Museum of South Texas, and Bayfront Plaza Convention Center, with its Selena Auditorium. Traveling exhibits at AMST, which was designed by noted architect Philip Johnson, have ranged from avant garde to Norman Rockwell.

Classes and exhibits of art work by local students are frequently on display on the ground floor.

The best view in town is from Harbor Bridge over the ship channel leading to Corpus Christi Beach. The harbor with tugs, cargo ships and tankers lies to the west, and Bayfront Plaza and the beach to the east.

A short distance north of Harbor Bridge, the USS Lexington Museum on the Bay dominates the skyline of Corpus Christi Beach. The Grand Old Lady's heroic history covers a big chunk of World War II, making the venerable old aircraft carrier the most distinguished veteran in town.

A variety of Navy aircraft is on display, but the ship itself with its colorful past is the main attraction. It was decommissioned at Pensacola, Fla., and towed to its berth near the jetties. Its keel is buried in the sand to give it stability.

This is particularly important in the event of a hurricane since the the Lex is no longer able to go to sea and to ride the storm out as Navy ships traditionally do.

Since history began, the Coastal Bend has been periodically buffeted by hurricanes. Oldtimers almost unthinkingly mark time by the hurricanes

Port of Corpus Christi

The submarine *USS City of Corpus Christi* pays a courtesy call to its namesake city. Thousands of residents went aboard to find out what an atomic submarine is like.

McGregor Collection-C.C. Museum

Repair crews work on a PBY, a Navy patrol bomber, in 1942 after it made a forced landing on an almost dry King Ranch water tank. Stripped of excess weight, it took off from the muddy pond with the help of a Ranch tractor and landed in the marina for repairs. Tragically, its crew members were killed when another plane returning them to California crashed.

Feed one seagull and it sends some sort of secret signal. Gulls over the horizon get the message and soon wing it to the food source, in this case a cruise-boat passenger who's finding out just what fearless and shameless beggars they are. Brown pelicans, returning from near extinction, are fast re-learning the art.

Sailboarders (right) take advantage of one of the local natural resources— the wind. Races attract international competitors, and the race across the bay and back offers a real test on a particularly windy day.

Part of the annual Buccaneer Days celebration involves forcing the mayor to walk the plank. These fierce pirates are celebrating His—or Her— Honor's splash.

they have experienced. Such storms do make a strong impression on the mind.

A severe blow hit the area in 1791, according to Mike Ellis' *Hurricane Almanac*, killing 50,000 cattle owned by Jose de la Garza Falcon, whose father established Santa Petronilla Ranch, 15 miles south of the Nueces River, 48 years before Corpus Christi was founded.

Several other storms that struck in the Brownsville area undoubtedly would have had

Esmeralda 'Lala' Salazar-Courtesy of Del Mar College

Schoolgirls (upper left) perform traditional Mexican dances at Bayfest, held each fall on Shoreline Boulevard. Other Shoreline celebrations include a summer Jazz Festival, Buccaneer Days in the spring, and *Cinco de Mayo*. Corpus Christi Bay hosts regattas and other sailing races year round.

(Upper right) This is a Hobie Cat race that started on the sands of Corpus Christi Beach.

No longer the 'USS' Lexington, since she is decommissioned, the ship's designation is not for a warship but for the USS Lexington Museum on the Bay. Exhibits are constantly added and upgraded.

effects had there been a settlement at the mouth of the Nueces River. A particularly violent one occurred in 1837. But Corpus Christi suffered only minor damage from those and a number of others until 1874, when the eye of a major storm passed directly over the city.

"Heretofore Corpus Christi has been exempt from desolation by the elements," *The Nueces Valley* reported. "We were mercifully spared. But now our time has come and we have had by far the most severe storm ever felt since this place was known as Kinney's Rancho." Docks were destroyed, homes damaged and a schooner was a half a mile inland.

"Water street is a thing of the past," the editor wrote. ". . . Half the chickens in Corpus Christi found an untimely fate."

Although no lives were lost and the city suffered no permanent damage, the storm did destroy one local industry: Tidal waters washed away the salt deposits that Corpus Christians had been harvesting for many years.

In 1880 a storm that struck Matamoros, Mexico, caused an eight-foot tide in Corpus Christi, flooding the town to the base of the bluff.

C.C. Public Library

(Above and right) Wreckage of the *Japonica* in 1919 and of a sailboat in 1980 show the fury of hurricanes. (Middle right) Debris in Hall's Bayou, now the ship channel, shows the strength of the 1919 storm. (Far right) A soldier (in 1919) and a National Guardsman (in 1970, after Hurricane Celia), stand guard to protect damaged property.

C.C. Caller-Times-Courtesy of C.C. Museum

In 1916 the tide rose to nine feet, destroyed most of the pleasure piers, and damaged waterfront structures. But Mayor Roy Miller had ordered evacuation of all low-lying areas, preventing loss of life in town.

In 1919 warning was desultory and the people complacent, resulting in terrible loss of life. That storm threatened to end all development on North Beach, so thoroughly were all structures swept away, among them some of the finest homes in the city.

Six blocks of the beach, an area owned by the King Ranch, was eroded inland some distance by the swirling tides. Later the ranch would deed its claim to the city with the proviso that the beach be open to the public.

Once more it was an ill wind that did good, for Corpus Christi Beach is not fenced off, posted against trespassers, as is land along so many bodies of water.

In 1933 twenty tropical disturbances were reported. Incredibly, seven of these made landfall between Corpus Christi and Tampico, Mexico. On September 5 of that year a storm killed 40 in Brownsville and caused considerable property damage on Corpus Christi's Bayfront, washing away North Beach's Pleasure Park Pier and The Ship, a sailing vessel that had been renovated into a dance pavilion.

The storm also wiped out the Don Patricio Causeway to Padre Island, making an island trip by automobile extremely difficult.

Starting in 1961 a succession of hurricanes acted as natural Urban Renewal projects, wrecking many substandard buildings. Others were damaged, condemned, and destroyed. Carla, in 1961, brought beachfront flooding. Beulah, in 1967, destroyed 178 dwellings; and Allen, in 1980, removed 210 structures.

Hurricane Celia, 1970, was a veritable tornado that wreaked half a billion dollars in insured wind damage but fortunately resulted in only 11 deaths. Fern, in 1971, was small but wet; and Allen, in 1980, heavily damaged boats, piers, marinas and structures on Corpus Christi Beach.

Hurricanes have a revitalizing effect on the environment by flushing out bays and estuaries and stirring up unhealthy deposits of silt.

They are harsh and cruel. They kill, maim and destroy. Yet they weed out the old and give the city a bright new face. For good or bad, they have made Corpus Christi the "Sparkling City by the Sea."

Courtesy of Mike Ellis

C.C. Public Library

C.C. Public Library

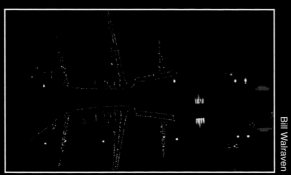

From the marina to the south to the air-craft carrier *Lexington* to the north, Christmas brings added sparkle to the Bayfront, while the Watergarden, framed by Harbor Bridge, glitters in any season. Sunrise brings a golden finish to a perfect night.

A Carancahua Indian, sculpted by Dr. Sherman Coleman, stands in the lobby of the Nueces County Courthouse. The Carancahuas were a tall, well-formed, uncompromising people. Wars and disease led to their extermination in the 1840s.

Bill Walraven

C.C. Public Library

Corpus Christi: Taylor-made from Kinney's Trading Post

Legend says that the first European to visit the Corpus Christi area was Spanish sea captain Alonso Alvarez de Pineda, who sailed along the Texas coast in 1519. Likely the next was Alvar Nunez Cabeza de Vaca, navigator for the ill-fated Panfilo de Narvaez expedition in 1527.

Three English seamen, set ashore after a sea battle at San Juan de Ullua, Mexico, in 1568, prob-ably passed by as they walked through the area on their way to Canada, but there was no such place as Corpus Christi when the Texas Land Office was created by the Congress of the Republic of Texas on February 1, 1838.

Two months later a band of surveyors led by James Manning drove in the first official survey stake near the shore of the bay in what is now Downtown Corpus Christi. John J. Linn had landed goods to smugglers here in 1829 and 1830, and H.L. Gilpin, a later resident, had done the same in 1832. Both reported no signs of habitation.

The Rev. Z.N. Morrell, an Indian fighter and a founder of the Baptist Church in Texas, accompanied the surveyors. He wrote:

Kinney

"Corpus Christi was the place where we

agreed to pitch our camp; a name simply given to a locality on our south western coast at the mouth of the Nueces River. We saw no indication of any former settlement at this place."

While the surveyors worked, Morrell and a companion went inland to explore the countryside. The friend took aim at an Indian boy they encountered, but the preacher ordered him not to fire. This act would save their lives.

They returned to camp to find Carancahua Indians had captured the surveyors. The boy they had spared was the son of the chief, who smiled, shook Morrell's hand, and returned the crew's horses and equipment.

Morrell wrote a letter for the chief to take to President Sam Houston, asking approval of a treaty with the tribe. At Victoria the party met the chief returning from Houston.

"The chief left us near Corpus Christi, almost naked. Now he stood before us, full six feet and four inches high, weighing 200 pounds, wearing a two-story silk hat, a fine broadcloth suit, and a fine pair of military boots, with a sword hanging at his side," Morrell wrote.

"He at once recognized our company and ran to shake hands, but on approaching me took me in his arms. This was the first and only Indian that ever hugged me.'"

This incident took place more than a year before Col. Henry L. Kinney and William P. Aubrey arrived to establish a trading post overlooking the bay. An ongoing Federalist revolution in Mexico created a lucrative market for illegal shipments of tobacco, gunpowder, shot, and other war materials. In return Kinney got saddles, blankets and bars of silver.

Corpus Christi had long been favored as a landing for smugglers, since it was isolated, difficult to reach by land or sea. Kinney proved quite proficient at the trade.

He is most often described as an "adventurer." The Pennsylvania native was suave, urbane and articulate. He loved fine brandy and women; the latter love contributed to his untimely end. Kinney dealt with Mexicans, Americans and Indians, walking a careful line to remain neutral.

When the country was overrun with "cowboys"—Anglo-American bandits enlisted as an informal militia—he exposed them to Mexican authorities.

Kinney had the ability to talk friends and perfect strangers out of their money. He conned Mexican Capt. Enrique Villarreal out of some 44,000 acres of land. Later, when he was in financial trouble, he didn't hesitate to mortgage again property he had already mortgaged.

Despite his faults, Kinney made a huge contribution to the history not only of Corpus Christi, but of the nation as well.

He drew colonists to Nueces County. He was the first to be concerned with a deep-water channel and moved to get such a project started. He built a small fort and maintained a small army on

Louis de Planque-Institute of Texan Cultures

C.C. Public Library

Capt. John Anderson's Swedish windmill stood on Water Street.

The Civil War Battle of Corpus Christi, August 17, 1862, was inconclusive, allowing both Union and Confederate forces to claim victory

the south end of the bluff. Then he built a pier between what are now Laguna and Starr Streets.

More importantly, he established a foothold with the only Nordic-controlled settlement south of the Nueces River, thus reinforcing the claims of both Texas and the United States to disputed territory above the Rio Grande. His information kept the United States abreast of what was going on in Mexico. He proved his bravery in battle and in saving shipwreck victims.

And when the Mexican War loomed, he was ready. Henry Kinney's fortunes soared in wartime. This was a new opportunity. To his delight, Corpus Christi became the center of the intense dispute between the United States and Mexico.

Kinney lobbied Maj. Andrew Jackson Donelson, U.S. envoy to Texas, to claim the Rio Grande as the boundary with Texas. He said that Corpus Christi should be the base for any military operation. Likely Gen. Zachary Taylor, who was given discretion to establish a base, chose Corpus Christi because it was in disputed territory but far enough from Mexican forces to allow him to prepare for the inevitable war.

The U.S. Army landed for the first time in Texas on St. Joseph's Island July 26, 1845, and on Corpus Christi Beach on July 31, making Corpus Christi Beach the first spot on the Texas mainland to fly the Stars and Stripes.

General Taylor's steam lighter, drawing only four feet of water, bogged down in a mudbank. After two uncomfortable steamy nights and plagued by mosquitoes, he agreed to pay local fishermen to take him ashore.

A New York journalist suggested the federal government should underwrite the cost of a channel into the bay. Corpus Christi newspapers would echo that cry over and over for three quarters of a century before it happened.

Taylor set up his headquarters on the beach between Bennett and Pearl Streets, about half a block north of the present site of the Texas State Aquarium.

The camp swelled from 2,000 to more than 4,000, representing more than half of the entire U.S. Army.

A list of the young officers who served here, most of them West Point graduates, sounds like a

C.C. Public Library

C.C. Public Library

The San Antonio and Aransas Pass Railroad causeway across the reef to Portland was built in 1886.

(Opposite page) An 1887 bird's eye view fancifully shows five trains and a bustling harbor.

(Middle left) Women's groups built a Ladies' Pavilion at the turn of the century for meetings, dances, plays, and skating parties.

The earliest view of the Bayfront is an India ink sketch made from a photo taken by Louis de Planque in 1874. Later that year a major hurricane altered the landscape. The flagpole marks the U.S. Customs House.

C.C. Public Library

Who's Who of Union and Confederate commanders in the Civil War.

Letters from soldiers indicated a bitter-sweet relationship with Corpus Christi. At first they were delighted. They could catch fish, turtles, crabs—a smorgasbord of seafood. The water was warm, the weather balmy. Were it not for the incessant drilling, firing practice and the fear of rattlesnakes in their tents at night, it would have been a great vacation.

The civilian population mushroomed from about 100 to several thousand. Saloons, gambling halls, bordellos, and other establishments suddenly appeared, all competing for the soldiers' money—$7 a month. Colonel Kinney was more than happy to supply horses and mules for the troops.

(There is no record explaining how Kinney received the title "Colonel." Apparently he gave it to himself.)

Capt. W.S. Henry, one of the first of Taylor's men to land, was overwhelmed by the pristine beauty of Corpus Christi before man wrought his hand on the landscape.

From the Bluff he saw "a view . . . magnificent in the extreme. Far off to the east the scene was bounded by whitecaps of the beautiful bay; to the southeast Flower Bluffs stood out in bold relief; in the northeast the distant highlands of Magloin's Bluff were dimly visible; to the northwest, the land near the mouth of the Nueces; in the west one unlimited plain. . . the home of the mustang and the buffalo.

"In the enthusiasm of the moment one might exclaim, 'It is God's favored land—the Eden of America.' When the enthusiasm subsided, it was not exactly that, but it certainly is very beautiful."

The honeymoon ended when winter came. The meager supply of firewood was a cooking problem. Latrines uphill from shallow water wells and other unsanitary camp conditions caused a serious outbreak of dysentery and a number of deaths. Finding drinking water was a problem.

Taylor ordered an artesian well dug, in what later became Artesian Park. Water from it was so sulphuric it was later considered therapeutic because "anything that tasted that bad must be healthy."

When northers hit, the men found that the tents leaked like sieves. Winter clothing was inadequate; and a shortage of firewood, making the wet soldiers even more miserable, caused even more illness. A soldier from Maine wrote that he had never been so cold at home.

General Taylor took up comfortable residence in a shellcrete house on Water Street.

When orders came to march to the Rio Grande, the army was more than ready to go. Taylor ordered that no camp followers or hangers-on were to go with the army, but many did tag along. Others left and the city was almost deserted.

At that time, eight years before Florence Nightingale made military nursing a respectable profession, untrained camp followers were performing such duties for Taylor's army in Corpus Christi.

THE MIRAMAR HOTEL, ON THE BEACH.

C.C. Caller-Times

Two magnificent hotels, Elihu Ropes' Alta Vista (opposite page) and the Miramar on North Beach. Economics killed the first and a fire the latter.

A newspaper nameplate fictionalizes the skyline. One view from the bluff and another from the bay show Corpus Christi before 1900.

CORPUS CHRISTI

CHRISTI, TEXAS, SUNDAY MORNING, APRIL 17, 189

C.C. Public Library

C.C. Public Library

C.C. Public Library

Concerts were held in the bandstand in Artesian Park, where water tasted so bad it was considered therapeutic.

Thousands gathered at Epworth by the Sea for Methodist camp meetings before a hurricane destroyed the facility.

View of Epworth League Grounds, Corpus Christi, Texas.

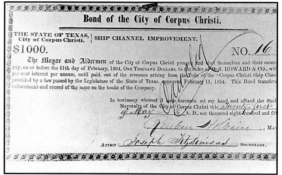

Taylor Street at the turn of the century showed the Church of the Good Shepherd and a grove of salt cedars that provided shade for tourists at Seaside Pavilion Hotel.

The city issued this municipal bond to pay D.S. Howard & Co. for dredging the ship channel. A toll was to repay the debt, but the job was never completed.

C.C. Public Library

C.C. Public Library

Two women, Mary Nolan and Sarah Borginnis, were listed as "matrons." Likely they were almost as medically qualified as the doctors, who managed through ignorance to kill almost as many soldiers as the enemy.

The famous Ranger Rip Ford described Sarah as a "giant of a woman with a man's stalwart frame, weighing over 220 pounds, who could whip any man, fair fight or foul. She could shoot a pistol better than anybody. She could outplay or outcheat the slickest of professional gamblers at blackjack."

She earned the title "Great Western" at Camp Marcy on the beach when a group of soldiers of the 6th Infantry was lounging against a building at the end of tent row. They noticed a woman bigger than any they had ever seen approaching. She had flaming red hair, which added to the illusion

of her height, already more than 6 feet. An awed soldier commented, "She's as big as the Great Western."

He was referring to an ocean-going steamship, the biggest afloat in that day. Unfortunately, his voice carried farther than he had intended. He didn't have a chance to say more, for the huge woman showed a quickness of foot totally unexpected of one so large. She lifted the man and slammed him against a shellcrete wall over her head. Then she held him there, with one hand.

The embarrassed soldier gasped and caught his breath. "I didn't mean no harm, Ma'am. I promise. It won't happen again."

She considered a moment, then accepted the apology and allowed him to fall to the ground.

Word spread through the camp. Nobody was

going to mess with Sarah Borginnis, but the wife of a 7th Infantryman earned a name that would follow her to her grave—"the Great Western."

At the fort that would become Fort Brown, she ignored flying shrapnel to minister to the wounded. She prepared and delivered food to the outnumbered troops and received a cannon pellet through her bonnet.

She followed the army south and often became a soldier, yet showed great tenderness in giving comfort to the wounded. She became a legend. By orders of General Winfield Scott, she was made a pensioner of the government. She died at Fort Yuma, Ariz., in December, 1866, and was buried with full military honors.

The other woman, Mary Nolan, had landed in New York with her two young brothers, Tom and

Matt. Their parents had sickened and died on the voyage from their native Ireland. In a strange land with no means of support, she was in a quandary until she saw an advertisement for U.S. Army matrons. She signed up and enlisted the boys, ages 10 and 12, as buglers. Apparently, they learned the required bugle calls on the voyage to Corpus Christi.

There wasn't much to do in the summer; but as winter approached, that changed. Matrons could only keep the patients clean and attempt to control their temperature. Mary undoubtedly learned much on the job.

The Nolans went south with the Army in the Mexican campaign. Mary returned to Corpus Christi, married Charles Hutchison and had two children. But she remained a nurse. Her husband died in the early 1850s, possibly in a yellow fever epidemic in 1854.

She nursed victims of that epidemic and sick soldiers in the Confederate hospital during the Civil War. She also worked night and day helping victims of a yellow fever epidemic in 1867.

An early resident said of her:

"She was one who was a real Angel of Mercy. All creeds, all colors alike. In sickness, death or trouble, it was never too cold or too stormy or too late to go to the sick and needy."

The two boys grew up to become Rangers and lawmen. Tom was killed by a drunken cowhand. Matt, sheriff and Confederate captain, won acclaim at Galveston, capturing a Union ship, and was promoted to lieutenant colonel for his actions at the Battle of Sabine Pass. He was gunned down by two assassins on Mesquite Street. Motive for the killing was never established. He and Tom are buried side by side in Old Bayview Cemetery.

After Taylor's army marched to the Rio Grande in the spring of 1846, residents were discouraged, but Henry Kinney the promoter was back, advertising the city as the gateway to the goldfields of California. And he had GI Surplus wagons to sell.

Corpus Christi in 1848 was scarcely as religious as its name indicated. It had gained notoriety as the Mexican War camp "where there were

few women and no ladies." It also received mention for its many saloons, brothels and gambling houses. Three years later that reputation was intact.

Corpus Christi Star Editor John H. Peoples—for whom Peoples Street was named—said a stranger had asked why "there is not a single place or house of worship in our beautiful little city."

The *Star* started a subscription for a church. It thought a school might be a good idea, too.

The following year the editor, crusading for social correctness, wrote, "'Excuse me,' as a friend of ours would say, for suggesting to our American and Mexican friends the propriety of going to our bay to perform their ablutions instead of the pond from whence most of the water, both for drinking and cooking, is obtained. It looks bad, and does not savor much of cleanliness."

The pond, near the beach, was fed by Chatham's Ravine, later Blucher Creek.

Mrs. Annie Moore Schwein, who was born as a slave in Corpus Christi in 1856, told in her recollections how the first church in the town came to

be built: "The preacher, a Rev. Lafferty, went to Old Man Peter Dunn (a Catholic) and asked for his help because the preacher was new here.

"Dunn finished pounding a horseshoe and took him to the Favorite Saloon, where he announced: 'Men, this man is trying to build a church for the people here. He needs some help to get the thing started. I want each of you to put the price of your next drink in this hat for the church.'

"The men stepped up and each contributed something. That was how the Methodist Church got started. . . It was a small adobe building facing south on Mann Street."

Later the Methodists returned the favor and helped their Catholic neighbors build a church.

Mormons, however, did not find the atmosphere so ecumenical. Two missionaries were holding meetings, for men only, in a waterfront warehouse when wives of some of the men interrupted the speaker by beating him with a dead cat. Others threw eggs and rotten vegetables at the pair. The wives declared the meeting adjourned, and the poor missionaries left town.

By 1854 progress was coming, with steamships arriving and wagon trains heading west. Then a fruit boat from Mexico brought a cargo of death. Yellow fever claimed at least one life in nearly every home in town. Some whole families were wiped out.

As the Civil War drew near, Kinney offered his services to President Lincoln. Getting no answer, he made the same offer to Confederate President Jeff Davis, but got the same result.

Kinney then went to Matamoros to recoup his fortunes. He made the mistake of calling on his former mistress. A shot was fired as he approached her house. Friendly editors reported him killed in battle, and he was buried in an unmarked grave.

Back in Corpus Christi Yanks and Rebels fought a battle that doesn't even qualify as a good skirmish in the larger scheme of the Civil War. Though the war was serious, sometimes it didn't seem so.

Casualties were so few and property damage from combat so relatively light that residents saw

humor in it, especially when Yankee cannon balls filled with good bourbon stored there by seamen rained down on the city.

Hundreds of shot hit houses, a cow, a St. Bernard. Through it all, one Rebel was killed, one wounded; one Yank slightly wounded. An attempted Union landing was beaten off. Newspapers on both sides claimed a great victory. J.W. Kittridge, a cocky and overconfident Union lieutenant, came ashore and was captured but was soon exchanged.

The actual fighting was the least of the problems. The Yankees blockaded the port, keeping goods out. A drought wiped out crops and gardens, a hard freeze killed drought-weakened cattle and fish in the bays. And there was danger from deserter brigands, bandits, Indians, and from constituted militia.

Mrs. Rosalie Hart Priour, returning from her classroom in town, found herself in the middle of a skirmish. As she was talking to Yankee guards, Confederates attacked.

"I had to walk through a shower of bullets," she wrote. "The battle continued until about 4

C.C. Caller-Times

A panoramic view of the Bayfront in 1907 shows four churches: First Presbyterian, left; St. Patrick's Cathedral, center; the Congregational Church, one of the first African-American churches in Texas, right; and the Church of the Good Shepherd, Episcopal. The photo was taken from the top of the Pavilion Hotel.

Photos-C.C. Public Library

Central Wharf.   CORPUS CHRISTI, Texas.

The *Pilot Boy* discharges a load of passengers at Central Wharf. The vessel sank in the 1916 hurricane with a loss of six lives.

Workers prepare the yacht *Margaret* for launch after drydocking. The three-master was a familiar sight in the bay in the early 1900s.

o'clock, but only two men were slightly wounded. It looked like children at play. The Confederates were on horseback and the Yankees on foot.

"One time Capt. Kittridge was pursued by a Confederate and lost his hat. Mr. Dunn picked it up and put it on his head, then chased him down the hill.

"A young lady, Miss Howell, ran after them as they passed her father's house clapping her hands and crying 'Hurrah! Hurrah, for the Confederates.'

"Capt. Kittridge returned to the charge. Mr. Dunn saw him coming, threw his own hat away but retained the one he had captured. Capt. Kittridge picked (Dunn's hat) up and put it on his head. The main thing the battle accomplished was an exchange of hats."

Early enthusiasm for the war faded. Harassment by the enemy and a lack of supplies made the duty trying. Then reinforced Union forces captured the local militia at Camp Semmes—now Port Aransas—November 17, 1863, and took them to prison in New Orleans.

Thus ended the Corpus Christi chapter of the War Between the States.

Union troops occupied the town for a time, but Reconstruction was not as harsh here as it was in other sections. Much of the population had been opposed to secession, including Edmund J. Davis, who would become, in Reconstruction, the first Republican governor of Texas. Many of the Union troops chose to make their home here.

One day in 1867 a stranger on horseback rode into town and became ill. Local people nursed him, and another yellow fever epidemic was touched off. One of every three residents of the village died. Many fled to the interior trying to escape, dying there and spreading the disease to other communities.

The *Advertiser* editor said, "A cloud of death hangs over our town."

Three doctors and five men of the cloth ministered to the sick and themselves died. Lumber

LOOKING SOUTH, DOWN BROADWAY.

C.C. Caller-Times

C.C. Public Library

Three days of snow paint the city white in 1887.

A steel engraving shows the view from the south end of Broadway in the early 1890s.

(Opposite top)With no boat basin available, small craft are rafted together for protection.

for a new Presbyterian church was used instead for caskets.

Davis, who had been a general in the Union Army of Texas, won the respect of his former enemies by rolling up his sleeves and nursing the sick night and day, at great risk to himself.

Mrs. Schwein recounted how he brought "Dr. Kearney here from Havana at his own expense after the three doctors, Merriman, Robertson and Johnson all died of the fever.

"Many mean things have been said about Mr. Davis," she said, "but he certainly deserves credit for what he did for Corpus Christi at that time...."

The plague also ended a fierce political battle for local offices. Death claimed too many officials and candidates. So many people died so rapidly that few were left to care for the sick and bury the dead. Domestic stock and dogs, with no one to care for them, ran wild in the streets. The town was left without local government, and a quarantine made recovery more difficult.

The next year the military commander appointed a local government which instituted harsh taxes. One, designed to remove a huge population of dogs from the streets, imposed a tax of one dollar for every puppy and male dog and two for each "slut."

Another ordinance decreed no one could keep more than three milch cows in town and provided a fine for those who milked cows other than their own. Yet another required owners of dead animals to remove the carcasses from the streets.

Owners were required to clean the stalls of horses, cows, hogs and other domestic animals in town by 8 a.m. daily.

Another concern was a reign of terror all over

Nueces County Historical Society

C.C. Public Library

(Opposite page) North Beach swimmers enjoy the slide. Women's bathing suits allowed no salacious showing of bare skin except the face and arms. Bathing suits did not become swimsuits until after World War I—perhaps styles changed after the boys got a good look at the attractions of Old Paree.

The panorama below shows the elegant old Nueces Hotel in 1913, the year it was completed. The picture was taken from the tower of the Beach Pavilion Hotel (left).

(Far right) A windmill pumped water for this slide opposite downtown.

The ladies below might as well go swimming. They're dressed for it, according to Queen Victoria.

(Bottom) A panorama view looking out to sea was taken about 1925, the year the breakwater was built.

(Middle) Covered piers, like the one from the newly completed Nueces Hotel, made privacy for modest maidens.

Texas. More than a thousand murders were reported over the state, many of them in Nueces County.

With limited access to the sea and the countryside alive with bandits, hostile Indians, and outlaws of every description, the city continued in a state of economic depression for a decade. Cattle theft and robbery remained the principal industries. The impasse was broken when the first railroad was begun in 1875. That year also marked

the last major bandit raid, which attacked Noakes Store near Calallen.

Industrial concerns on the Bayfront date from those early days, when there was a dispute over fees charged by the city at the Municipal Wharf built by Kinney and William Mann. The city insisted on 30-year leases at what others considered exorbitant prices. Norwick Gussett built his own wharf on North Beach, and for years his two

Central Wharf - March 3rd 1908

"Fishing on C.C. Bay -"

C.C. Public Library

Caller-Times

large schooners were major shippers. Others followed suit and built piers for their own use.

At that time Corpus Christi definitely was not a tourist town. Starting soon after the Mexican War, packeries around the bay rendered cattle for tallow and hides. Packery owners had the political clout to operate as they pleased, so much unsold beef was dumped into the bay, along with other unused animal body parts.

Naturally there was no incentive for anyone to swim in the bay. Corpus Christi definitely had an air about it.

There was a butcher shop in Market Hall. Smells from the hide warehouses on the waterfront and from rotting carcasses in the water produced an assault on the olfactory senses that no modern industry could equal. The City Council, bowing to citizen pressure, passed an ordinance forbidding throwing of fish heads, animal entrails and other waste into the streets or on Market Square. Add to this the swarms of flies and mosquitoes and you have a city that was truly a last resort.

Men returned from the Civil War to find the ranges overrun with cattle. Trail drivers drove some herds to rail heads in the Midwest; but there was no market for so much beef.

Photos-C.C. Public Library

During those years hide and wool warehouses made the Bayfront port a busy place. Bales of hides weighing a ton or so were shipped out. The port also became for a brief decade the biggest wool shipping port in the nation.

By 1875, however, there was a shortage of cattle. Barbed wire, windmills and railroads brought people and prosperity and changed the countryside.

Corpus Christi desperately needed deeper channels to become a city, but the struggle to expand shipping operations from the Bayfront to a deepwater port was an arduous and frustrating process that would take three-quarters of a century to accomplish.

Starting with Kinney, who bought a dredge-boat, something always seemed to go wrong. If it wasn't lack of money, it was lack of all governmental support.

The Civil War had ended one attempt to cut a channel. The dredge had opened a shallow channel through the mudbanks when Union sailors burned it to the waterline. Then local citizens decided they didn't want a channel to provide a path for Union invaders, so they sank a boat filled with concrete in the new channel. A Union steamboat easily pulled their boat aside. Another local boat was fleeing from Yankee invaders when the crew attempted to blow it up. Unfortunately for them, they set a fuse to a sack of brown sugar and carried the powder ashore. The opened channel allowed the Union to bombard the city.

In 1874 the Morris and Cummings Co. dredged a channel west of Harbor Island. The entire area welcomed the *Gussie*, a sea-going steamer, when it docked at Municipal Wharf. A

Photos-Courtesy of Dean Thorpe

water street just around the corner from home

Photos-Courtesy of Mike Ellis

Aug. 16 - 1916

The Beach Pavilion stands alone after the 1916 storm wiped out the rest of the pier. Three years later it would not be so lucky.

(Left opposite) Cotton bales are loaded aboard the bay steamer *Pilot Boy* for shipment to a freighter off Harbor Island.

(Middle opposite) The popular cruise boat *Japonica* is shown at sea and then swamped at its dock during the 1916 hurricane.

(Bottom opposite) A North Beach rail washout from the same storm. Another craft was washed ashore over Water Street.

new day had arrived. Two years later Morgan Line steamers were dragging bottom and Corpus Christi was once more host to shallow draft vessels only.

The Texas-Mexican Railroad to Laredo was finished in 1881. The maiden trip of the "Manana Express," as it came to be known, has to be one of the most memorable on record.

Captains Richard King and Mifflin Kenedy, greatest contributors to the railroad's construction, invited all the notables along the line.

The excursionists included doctors, bankers,

lawyers, judges, preachers, deacons, vestrymen, bishops, citizens, ranchers, and other leaders of Nueces, Duval and adjoining counties. The date was September 27, 1881.

District Attorney D. McNeill Turner, son of a minister, was chosen to prepare the lemonade. His concoction included pineapple and other fruit juices to formulate Roman punch. Turner and his assistants went to consult with others about the contents. While they were gone, parties unknown added three gallons of alcohol and 12 quarts of champagne to the barrel of brew, making "a most excellent type of Roman punch."

The day was unusually warm and the assemblage was thirsty.

"By the time the train arrived at Pena Station a state of hilarity manifested itself," one account said. "When the band reached Laredo, members of the band were stretched out on the seats sound asleep, while some of the most prominent excursionists were in charge of the instruments and making such a noise that when the train rolled into Laredo, many of the people of that city thought the world was coming to an end."

Someone, thought to have been Judge James O. Luby of San Diego, wrote an epic poem nam-

After the 1919 storm rescuers turned out before the water receded on Peoples Street.

Debris piled up on Mesquite Street illustrates the fury of the storm tide.

(Opposite page) Workers search for bodies immediately after the hurricane.

ing the victims of the prank who themselves would ever after laugh at the recollection. A few of the verses are enough to illustrate the tone of the epic:

"... Alfred Evans then to a point of order arose.

While addressing the guards in classic pose,

On Allen Davis's sombrero he skinned his nose.

On the Excursion to Laredo.

With the Medical Corps Hamilton quietly sat.

Doctor Spohn on the drum played rat-ta-tat, Doctor Turpin mourning the loss of his hat On the Excursion to Laredo.

Long life to Captain King and Kenedy, too. And Col. Hungerford who put us safely through,

To all of them our lasting thanks are due, For our pleasant trip to Laredo."

Strangely enough, some merchants opposed the railroad, saying it would diminish a profitable hide and wool trade conducted by ox cart. But those industries had already declined. Shortly after the turn of the century, after the railroads had opened South Texas to farming, the port became a major exporter of cotton.

However, the bar at the Gulf into Aransas Pass shoaled over until 1899, when jetties were installed and a channel dredged. In 1910 the

Photos-Courtesy of Mike Ellis

The lonely shell of the North Beach home of Judge J.D. McDonald stands as one of the few remains of the finest subdivision in Corpus Christi. Tides remained high a day after the storm. Only the old Beach Hotel survived the tidal onslaught.

Army Corps of Engineers approved a port at Harbor Island near the Gulf, a cheaper alternative to one at Corpus Christi. These facilities would be destroyed in a 1916 storm, setting up a new game.

On the brighter side, the decline of the packeries renewed a realization that people might pay to come to the coast for sunshine, bathing, fishing, boating and hunting.

As early as 1885 local enthusiasts had bragged on the continuous, cooling seabreezes, lying that there were no marshes hereabouts where mosquitoes might breed.

The spiel had improved the next year with the claim: "Winds prevent the possibility of the accumulation of noxious vapors or disease germs, and furnish a perpetual supply of the purest air from the ocean."

And "Rainfall is constant and always around when you need it."

Henry Kinney was a promoting piker compared to the sewing-machine salesman who blew into town in 1890 and created the city's biggest boom and the biggest bust.

Col. Elihu H. Ropes might have succeeded with his subdivision, super hotel, street cars, railroad, and channel to the Gulf had not the national economic panic of 1893 sent him packing, leaving the town broke and depressed.

The approach of a new century offered more

C.C. Museum

The area near Hall's Bayou—later the ship channel—suffered almost as much damage as North Beach.

Tides swept across the bayou into Nueces Bay with tremendous force. Debris like that on Chaparral Street was driven by mountainous waves, pounding victims in the water. Many were knocked unconscious and drowned.

C.C. Public Library

hope. A new port at Port Aransas, railroads, a flood of tourist and immigrants made the future seem bright. In 1899 a newspaper story asked, "Wonder What They Will Do Next? They have opened a public station at Fivel's Restaurant, putting a slot machine in a large booth where anyone at any hour can stop in and talk to any part of the city for a nickel or to points hundreds of miles away without having to go to Central. . ."

Remains of Spohn Hospital north of the present-day ship channel. Heroic nuns saved many patients as the building crumbled around them.

Many boats were washed inland.

Workers sort rubble below undamaged homes. People living safely above the Bluff had no idea of the storm's ferocity until they awoke the next morning to the horror below.

Courtesy of Mike Ellis

A beach landmark of that period was Epworth-by-the-Sea, a Methodist camp. Local civic leaders had donated 15 acres and a 10,000-gallon water tank to the group. Thousands of people came every summer to the Epworth League encampment, where a strict code of Victorian morality was enforced. It was a self-contained city, complete with its own barber shop, ice cream parlor, cold drink stands, news stands, club room, restaurants, laundries, post office, and railroad station, where special trains unloaded. The Epworth crowds reminded local boosters of the value of tourism, and tourism advertising increased.

The seafood industry also began to develop. With the coming of the railroads, barrels of iced seafood could be shipped to metropolitan markets; and the fish and oyster industry grew rapidly on the north end of the beach. There was also a market for the mountains of oyster shells that accumulated. Since most of the streets in town were unpaved, ground oyster shell was a fine substitute for pavement.

Many structures and sidewalks in early Corpus Christi were made of shellcrete—ground seashells and sand. Lime in the shells hardened the substance into a product as durable as any modern concrete. Local restaurants specialized in oysters, fish, turtle and wild game. Strangely, since the bays were teeming with them, the menu didn't include shrimp. People generally didn't think they were good to eat—many thought they were some sort of insect.

Theodore Fuller, who played on the beach as a child, netted shrimp and brought them home after someone told him they were good for something other than bait. His mother cooked his shrimp, boiling them so long they resembled rubber. This confirmed her view that shrimp were not fit for human consumption. She fed them to the chickens, who found them delicious.

Then a packer included shrimp in a ship-

Courtesy of Mike Ellis

A National Guardsman walks past a flag-draped body in the debris. The Nueces County Courthouse is in the background.

After the storm a mountain of cotton bales clogged the downtown area.

A great many people felt they would be safer remaining in their own houses. Survivors told of staying home to put furniture, keepsakes, and other valuables at a safe level. Then it was too late to leave. This woman remained and survived.

(Far right) Waves alone would not have been so dangerous; but lumber, pilings, and other debris plowed into houses and turned them into broken wreckage to compound the carnage. The tide, once it started, rose at a remarkable pace. Many had crossed the railroad trestle over Hall's Bayou, a small stream between North Beach and town, a route they had used in 1916. In 1919 the stream quickly became a raging torrent. Of those who tried to swim for it, some made it. Others drowned, and a few brave men also drowned trying to save them.

ment of fish, and European immigrants in Chicago discovered that Corpus Christi Bay was a treasure trove of big scrumptious shrimp waiting to be steamed, boiled, fried, barbecued, or simmered in creole or gumbo. Suddenly local citizens found out what they'd been missing, and a new industry was born.

Royal Govens had a fish and turtle cannery on North Beach. He canned turtle soup and kept turtles in pens and fed them raw beef, then tying the turtles' legs and shipping them live. His canned turtle and terrapin were sold in Baltimore.

People in those early days weren't exactly environmentally friendly. They considered sea bird eggs fair game and killed off pretty birds to sell their feathers, which brought a hefty price in the East, where big feathered hats were the vogue. Another practice oldtimers recalled would be even more intolerable today. In the days before boats had motors, "sports" would harpoon a porpoise and allow the wounded creature to pull the boat around the bay. This usually spelled death for the poor porpoise.

The oldtimers also found curlews, sandhill cranes, and likely whooping cranes to be tasty meals. Fishermen slaughtered thousands of young brown pelicans because they thought pelicans were eating the fish they weren't catching.

In those days street peddlers sold oysters for 25 cents a bucket. The city passed an ordinance requiring lids on the buckets. One vendor was puzzled that he was making absolutely no sales. Since he didn't understand English well, he didn't know that the bucket he bought with a lid on it was a chamber pot (the receptacle kept under the bed at night to forestall a trip to the outdoor privy).

In 1907, the Board of Trade trumpeted, the city had three railroads; a beautiful bay affording fine bathing, sailing and fishing; a 15-ton capacity ice factory; 30 automobiles; and 15 gasoline launches.

When the Nueces Bay Causeway was completed in 1912, people welcomed it with joy. It was not just another bridge. It was as great as getting indoor plumbing, maybe better.

From the earliest days the only way to cross the bay to the north of the city was by negotiating a series of reefs.

On February 26, 1747, Indian guides had led Joaquin de Orobio y Basterra, then captain of the Presidio of La Bahia, and a troop of 50 men across that underwater bar as he explored south to the Rio Grande.

Basterra described the land between the San Antonio and Nueces Rivers as beautiful and well watered, with grass and woods suitable for settlement.

Later travelers followed stakes driven along the edges of the crossing known as "The Reef."

They had no problem, unless weather had knocked down the stakes or pranksters rearranged them, perhaps to dunk—horse, wagon, and all—a family in Sunday finest on the way to Mass across the bay.

The stakes were inspected regularly, and vandals who tampered with them could find themselves in a real heap of trouble.

The new causeway opened North Beach to a flood of tourists. Strangers, naturally, had not wanted to trust their luck in driving their wheels across the bay waters.

The proud new causeway was heavily damaged in 1916 and destroyed in 1919. A wooden,

Photos-Courtesy of Mike Ellis

Rescue workers scour debris outside the Nueces Hotel. Hundreds were saved because they made it to that sturdy building.

Corpus Christi has "come back"

OFFICE OF THE GOVERNOR
Austin, Texas

Wednesday, Nov. 26, 1919

To the People of Corpus Christi:

E MERGING TRIUMPHANT *from the severest test of your endurance, you face a future that may be made alluring by lofty vision and by the strength of your will molded into a monument of lasting greatness.*

With a steadfastness of heroic courage, the persistency of indefatigable labor, the pride of home and family, the ambition of forward-looking Americans animating the lives and purpose of your citizenship, you cannot fail. These qualities I know you possess. They shall electrify the endeavors of the ensuing years and burn away the barrier to your progress.

Texas and America, yea the civilized world, admires the resolution of your spirit, sympathize with you in the trials of your task and prophesy for you the accomplishment of building up from the ashes of your ancient glory a future that shall surpass the grandeur of the past and become the mark of advancing prestige, abiding happiness and spiritual and material wealth. You are the master of your fate; you are the captain of your soul. For Texas I congratulate you upon your indomitable spirit and express confidence in your enduring victory over grief and dreadful circumstances.

WILLIAM P. HOBBY,
Governor of Texas.

Nueces County Historical Society

Governor William P. Hobby's message of encouragement reinforced the people's determination to rebuild and turn the disaster to their advantage. Hobby was the son of Alfred N. Hobby, whose 8th Texas Infantry was involved in the Battle of Corpus Christi.

more temporary, structure was built to replace it. That one had to be patched up after the 1933 hurricane. The temporary structure served another 25 years until it was finally replaced by a single concrete structure and much later by a multi-lane span.

Shortly after the first causeway opened, prohibition brought bitter divisions to the city. The tourist industry hit a snag in 1915 when two prohibition evangelists hit town. Mordecai F. Ham did the preaching and William J. Ramsey the singing, and thousands came to their revivals in a huge tent.

At the time Corpus Christi had 37 saloons, gambling halls, and houses of prostitution.

A poll tax drive and petitions led to an election March 16, 1916. In the campaign thousands crowded the bayfront to hear Ham and Ramsey harangue from a wagon bed.

Fist fights broke out between men, and girls tore campaign ribbons from the dresses of former friends. Women couldn't vote, but they were so active they were a dominant force in the election.

They'd shown their power the year before, when they got an ordinance passed ordering all saloons on Chaparral, Mesquite, and Water Streets to move to the east side of the street so that ladies could walk the sidewalks without having to peer into the awful dens of sin.

Merchants who tried to stay neutral on the wet-dry issue were threatened with boycott.

Some 92 percent of the men voted. A heavy turnout in small towns in the county carried the dries to victory by 218 votes out of a total of 3,377 cast. It was many months before half the population was speaking to the other half.

Early in the century the Bayfront was an especially fine place for boys to play. They had guns, slingshots, knives. They built their own boats and hunted and fished, practically in downtown.

Boys could earn four cents a pound for the lead contained in rifle balls fired at targets by Zachary Taylor's army on the beach.

"After a rain, sand washed from under them, leaving them on a little peak. . ., like a golf ball on a tee," one oldtimer recalled.

Another remembered playing on embankments thrown up during the Mexican War.

"We found the Army garbage dump," he said. "There were old skillets, canteens, knives and forks from 1845. Today they'd make fine museum pieces."

In the days before World War I, when Pancho

The city needed a deep-water port for progress and a seawall for storm protection. Civic leaders seized the moment to get both, with the help of all South Texas. North Beach jetties to serve as a breakwater were one immediate result.

(Above left) A train pulls carloads of granite boulders into the bay on rails installed specifically for that purpose. The boulders made a breakwater to protect the beaches and small craft on the Bayfront from rough water. This was in 1925.

The Pier Cafe was a fixture for years at the base of the Pleasure Pier in front of the Nueces Hotel.

McGregor Collection-C.C. Museum

With the Port of Corpus Christi in the background, the Bascule Bridge was a familiar landmark. The bridge was raised and lowered as many as 40 times a day. A tender operated it from the white structure on the bridge.

(Middle) Pilings are driven for raised warehouses in the new port.

(Opposite page) The destroyer Claxton, a World War I four-piper, was one of many military ships that have visited over the years.

(Bottom) The breakwater was originally a line of protective boulders. A concrete walk was added to make it one of Texas' premier fishing spots.

Villa and other raiders were threatening the border, the Cole Park area was briefly an Army camp. In 1917 soldiers bivouacked in that area went to the firing range on North Beach, in the same area where Taylor's troops had target practice across the salt flats.

Teachers at David Hirsch School were hard put to keep students in their seats as soldiers practiced firing machine guns outside their classroom windows.

For years little boys recovered rifle balls they used for fishing weights and missiles for their slingshots in the flats after rains uncovered them.

It was a peaceful, small-town existence, but darker, more foreboding clouds were on the horizon. A hurricane caused major damage on the Bayfront in 1916, but that was nothing compared to what would occur three years later.

The worst event in Corpus Christi history— the Great Storm of 1919—struck on September 14. Years later survivors recalled the horror of the day.

Jonnie Fifer, then 14-year-old Jonnie Brock, was having dinner with her family and a couple

from Tennessee when her father decided the water was too deep to drive to town. Suddenly "the wall peeled off like it was one board.

"We were holding hands when a wave knocked us apart," she said. "I never saw any of them again. A wall came by and I put my arm through a little window and held on."

All night long she held on, praying as she strangled, hit by debris. The next morning "a lady feeding her chickens saw me wade out of the

water. My long hair was plastered down and I was bruised and cut. She said, 'Lands sakes, child. Where in the world did you come from?'

"It was a farm outside Odem. I had floated nearly 20 miles. It was the first they knew how bad the storm was. They took me to town to see a girl's body. It was a girl I went to school with."

She was taken to live with her grandmother in Collin County. She wouldn't return to Corpus Christi for 60 years.

Her mother, father, twin sisters and baby brother were dead. When she came back, the only grave she could locate was that of her mother.

Before the storm Eulalio G. Vela had a wife, seven young children—two boys and five girls— and a good house on North Beach.

"The day after the storm," he recalled, "I had nothing. On Sunday the wind started blowing. I had never seen wind blow with such fury. The house shook.

"We went to a stronger house. It was not much better. The water hit it with a great roar. It

Photos-McGregor Collection-C.C. Museum

(Top) A four-masted schooner clears the Bascule Bridge as it leaves the port. Note the aft mast doubled as a smokestack for an auxiliary engine.

Thousands of people endure a long wait to board 'Old Ironsides,' the *USS Constitution*, on a 1932 visit to the Port of Corpus Christi.

went to pieces which were swept out to sea as you would scatter corn to chickens."

He grabbed a telephone pole, but it kept turning over and over. Lumber and debris hit him, nearly knocking him unconscious. A door with a

hole in it hit him, and he put his head and shoulders through the hole. He figured his body would be found if he stayed in the door.

He was battered and bruised, his eyes swollen shut. He floated into a hill and fell asleep. Later he

No need to ask where the fish were in December 1932. They were in deep water in the channel just outside the new harbor.

The Pier Cafe was relocated for an improved Pleasure Pier.

(Right) Looking south on Water Street in 1934, you would see San Antonio Machine and Supply Co. on a landfill pier that became the L-Head.

(Opposite page) This is the Bayfront as viewed from the end of the Pleasure Pier in 1930. After 1941 this was the view from the Peoples Street T-Head.

Photos-McGregor Collection-C.C. Museum

Caller-Times

Courtesy of Mike Ellis

A 1933 hurricane did little except flood streets around town but created havoc on North Beach.

and another survivor found a skiff and sailed to Calallen. Forty days later he went back and picked up the door. He kept it near the front of his restaurant all his life. He married again and had five children.

His son Felix kept the door with the faint lettering still on it:

"In Remembrance of Sept. 14, 1919."

Just before the arrival of the storm, Col. Theodore Fuller remembered, the fish were biting furiously. Flounder were so thick people were gigging them with cooking forks and umbrellas.

His father and an older brother left to search for a safe house. The rest of the family waited too long, and the tide came up suddenly. His mother and her sister had taken time to roll up carpets and put them upstairs. Then they took shelter in a nearby house. They barely got out before it exploded. A soldier helped them but was injured and sank beneath the waves.

Theodore, his sister, Esther, his Aunt Doshie, and a friend, Billy, climbed on a raft, but it fell apart. The aunt drowned. Waves carried wreckage of houses, piers, boats that kept falling on them. Wind was shrieking, poles, planks, furniture hitting them. Billy washed away and drowned.

Esther kept young Theodore's head above water most of the night. When he awoke, they were floating in calm water, across Nueces Bay, after 18 hours in the water. Three days later his father came to Sinton by train and found the two. He told them their brother had survived. His mother?

"He looked over me with his eyes on the horizon as he answered. Papa had a clear, deep voice which was soothing," Fuller said. "No, son, she is with Aunt Doshie and we won't see them for a long, long, time. They are in heaven."

Of the 12 people in the house, three sur-

McGregor Collection-C.C. Museum

The 1930s decade was the heyday of North Beach. It was a small-scale Six Flags Over Texas, with an amusement park that had a roller coaster, a Ferris Wheel, and other rides and entertainment. Its bathhouse rented sanitized wool bathing suits, and the saltwater pool was free of jellyfish. Swimming and diving competitions and beauty contests were held there, and holidays drew thousands for air shows, boat races, and other attractions. North Beach was the place to be, especially on July 4.

McGregor Collection-C.C. Museum

vived—Esther, a Mr. Carpenter, and 10-year-old Theodore.

Annis Reid lived in a sturdy house on Chaparral Street—near where the ship channel is today. The house shook and Percy Reid decided to take their 6-year old son to safety. Before he could return for his wife, the house disintegrated. She fell into the water and was swept away. Before she could sink, her young collie, Scotch, grabbed her by the hair and pulled her to a make-shift raft. She couldn't swim.

Time after time waves dumped them into the water. Each time Scotch pulled her back. She was pounded by tin, nails and posts. About 2 a.m. they were knocked into the water. She grabbed the raft but couldn't find her faithful dog. She washed ashore at White Point.

"I had taken my dress and petticoats off to keep from sinking," she said. "All I had on was one bone hairpin, and it was broken."

She found a shack, crawled into a cotton sack,

An aerial view shows the popularity of the North Beach Amusement Park. Note the stadium (right center) was the famous saltwater swimming pool.

The boatworks was a thriving business just across the channel.

Splash Days and later Buccaneer Days beauty pageants were held on the beach.

Surf was smaller; but access to Padre Island was limited, so North Beach was the choice.

Photographer 'Doc' McGregor shot this view from the top of the Bascule Bridge.

The Princess Louise Hotel, later La Posada Apartments, was next to the water.

and went to sleep. In the morning a girl gathering eggs found her and screamed. She was put on a horse and taken to Taft.

Of 15 people in the house who were carried across the bay, only three survived. She never forgot her heroic collie who lost his life saving hers.

E.J. Kilmer, a cabinet maker, built a fine home on the water near Palo Alto Street. Salt cedars he planted along the shoreline became a favorite shady retreat for tourists.

He built a pier out from his house and put a cottage on it. A distant cousin of Joyce Kilmer, the famous author of the poem "Trees," he wrote humorous rhymes.

After the 1916 storm destroyed his pier and cottage, he repaired the damage to his private park. In August 1919 a visitor offered him $10,000 for his home.

"I would never sell that house for any amount of money. It is my heaven on earth," he said.

He was in New York when the storm razed the structures on the bayfront. He refused to believe his home was gone.

He came home, viewed the desolation, and took to his bed. There was no longer any poetry in his soul. Three weeks later he was dead of a broken heart.

Clyde Prather recalled that the wireless at the Army hospital reported on Friday before the storm that it had hit Key West.

"As gusts of wind picked up, a Mr. Harden, who owned Harden's Courts, said Key West had been wiped off the face of the earth. He thought we should get to higher ground," Prather said.

As water rose, a policeman told him he didn't think they were in any danger.

C.C. Public Library

(Opposite page) **The port began importing automobiles in the mid-1930s. Dry cargo was important early, but tonnage in petroleum and chemicals soon dominated.**

In 1937, Pleasure Pier festivities involved shrimp boats.

This 1934 photo of the skyline on a calm day shows the White Plaza Hotel on the Bluff as the city's tallest structure.

Caller-Times

An aerial view looking down Mesquite Street to the south shows downtown in the 1930s. Note that the Princess Louise, on the water's edge to the left, was under construction.

(Bottom right) This statue of Christ was designed for the Bayfront by famed Mount Rushmore sculptor Gutzon Borglum, but it was rejected. His son, Lincoln Borglum, displays the model.

(Opposite) Leading city hotels as pictured by the Chamber of Commerce in the 1930s. In the 1990s two —the Hoover and the Princess Louise, by then, condos—still stood.

C.C. Public Library

The water rose quickly. Only with the aid of a soldier were they able to get out to the courthouse as a man came running and said, "They're drowning like flies down there."

People were hanging onto rooftops. Houses were being washed away. The next day bodies, all covered with thick black oil, were spread on the courthouse lawn. About 2 in the afternoon the water was a foot deep on Water Street where D.N. Wright lived.

"I called the Weather Bureau and they said the worst was over," he said. "If we were in a sturdy house, stay there. I called my relatives on the Beach and told them that. They had started to drive to town, but they turned back. My grandparents on both sides, aunts, uncles and cousins drowned—nine altogether.

"Water flowed down Belden Street so we couldn't cross to the courthouse. Men on the courthouse grounds formed a human chain to keep from being swept away. They stretched across the street and pulled us across."

Corpus Christi's Hotels are modern in every respect. Some of them are located on the Bay shore, while the others are only a few blocks from the water's edge.

Courtesy of Robin Borglum Carter

Others said the food supply ran out in the courthouse and there was no food for infant refugees. Suddenly a cow appeared, struggling in the water. They took her up to the second floor, and she provided an emergency supply of very fresh milk for the babies.

Malcolm Lee Purcell, who lived in Robstown, was visiting the Carl Blucher home when the hurricane hit.

He said the Weather Bureau had been reporting a storm for eight days. It crossed southern Florida and went straight west. Then it was reported touching the Louisiana coast.

Mr. Blucher, at work in his ice and electric plant on Water Street, had not returned. They assumed he had taken shelter in the Nueces Hotel. Water had reached the foot of the bluff. About 4:30 a.m. Blucher came home, soaking wet, pale and shaken. He could have left his plant, but the wife of an employee refused to leave. As the building broke up, they crawled into an empty ammonia tank and floated free. They drifted nearly all night until the waters receded enough for them to wade out.

"All brick buildings stood, while nearly all wooden buildings were wrecked. Lumber, cotton, boats, logs, stock from the stores, dead bodies of men and beasts were strewn all over the downtown district," Purcell said.

"Crude oil blackened everything, but it may have served as a disinfectant and saved the city from sickness following the flood."

Dr. W. E. Carruth and his family were in his sanitarium on North Beach when the water suddenly began to rise. Their situation looked hopeless until a 24-foot sailboat washed over the fence and into the yard.

Just as the Carruths and visitors, a total of 13 people, boarded the boat, his building collapsed. The emergency crew found four buckets and bailed water from the boat until it landed on the south shore of Nueces Bay.

Carruth was convinced that God sent the boat.

Miss Lucy Caldwell, a schoolteacher from Terrell, was staying in the Nueces Hotel during the

storm. She said that water on Chaparral Street was 10 1/2 feet deep. She was assigned by the Red Cross to the courthouse to help serve food and distribute clothing to refugees. In a letter she described her experiences:

"I saw Mexicans, Negroes, and Whites all huddled together, hungry, almost naked, barefooted....women with their hair down, some with toes cut off, hands cut off, teeth knocked out, limbs broken or cut ... women shrieking for lost ones, men prostrated from trying to save their families....

"Rescue parties came in every hour or two... sometimes with as many as 20 bodies. And, oh,

McGregor Collection-C.C. Museum

The skyline grew in the 1940s as the Robert Driscoll Hotel neared completion on Upper Broadway.

Smoke drifts from two steamers in the tiny turning basin. SAMSCO was on the Municipal Wharf (bottom), now the L-Head.

W.E. Pope Papers-Special Collections & Archives-Bell Library-Texas A&M University-CC

Water Street got its name from its location—right on the water's edge. This building was built as an Eagles Lodge, then was used by the Boy Scouts. It became The Dragon Grill, then the Town Club, and in the 1980s and 1990s a series of restaurants, including a grill and brew pub. The Princess Louise Hotel, seen in the background, was still standing in the 1990s, converted into condominiums.

Workers repair a line on the edge of Water Street near the Princess Louise Hotel. Riprap protected the street from erosion.

The Lone Star Grocery was located on a pier over the water, but dredge material brought it to ground level.

McGregor Collection-C.C. Museum

Caller-Times

the condition they were in, arms and legs off, heads almost severed, all the hair gone, swollen beyond conception and black from the oil. . . .

"And the odor cannot be described in words. Slime, mud, dead horses along the beach, decayed fruits and vegetables, burst sewers, wet lumber, molded dry goods. The streets were so slippery with slime from the oil. . . you could not hope to go many feet without slipping down. . . ."

She ended her letter by saying, "P.S. I have avoided telling you the most horrible things I saw."

Responsibility for such horror is difficult to assess. The people had warning, but the Weather Bureau was not emphatic about ordering evacuation because its information, correctly received, did not place the winds at dangerous levels.

What was not known was that the storm was moving slowly, pushing a tremendous tidal swell ahead of it. Ocean geologist Dr. Armstrong Price said this tidal wave effect is diminished when a storm comes in at an angle.

People were slow to react, even when the tides began to rise rapidly. Finally, they had developed a false sense of security from history and from what they had been told.

On September 29, 1886, the *Corpus Christi*

Caller had said, "The *Caller* has always contended that Corpus Christi, with its beautiful high bluff, is the only really safe place on the coast of Texas, and we are more convinced of this fact now than ever. This is the only seaport city with high ground, and where there is not the least danger of being swept into the sea."

Later, on July 3, 1909, the *Caller* bragged, "The hurricane tidal wave at Point Isabel, with hardly a blow here, emphasizes the perfect exemption of Corpus Christi from such natural cataclysms. The oldest inhabitants cannot recall a storm of sufficient severity to alarm even a timid woman and were this not so, the configuration of the islands separating the bay from the Gulf is such to preclude the possibility of a tidal wave sweeping over Corpus Christi. Besides this. . . nine-tenths of the area of Corpus Christi is on a bluff thirty feet high—the highest point on the Gulf Coast. Probably the safest point on saltwater in America."

After the tragedy of the 1919 hurricane, a "safe harbor" was deemed necessary. Corpus Christi had finally won the long struggle, beating out Aransas Pass as a new metropolis, the gateway to the Southwest.

The Port of Corpus Christi was good for the city, but it needed just a little help, like discoveries of vast pools of oil. Almost immediately, the tiny port was inadequate as the outlet for local oil refineries, chemical plants, and ore refineries, as well as the bountiful crops of corn, cotton, and milo maize.

Such prosperity caused the population to double and double again, in unprecedented spurts of growth.

Even so, all was not peaceful among the natives during the 1920s. A bitter dispute arose among Ku Klux Klan members and anti-Klan forces.

The issue was not race, the subject for which the Klan was notorious throughout the South. It was a religious schism between Catholics, which the Klan opposed, and non-Catholics.

The controversy was not limited to Corpus Christi. Nationally, the anti-Catholic fervor would peak in the 1928 presidential campaign, when Republican Herbert Hoover defeated the Catholic Democratic candidate, Al Smith.

Fear that a Catholic president would enable

Kilgore Collection-Special Collections & Archives-Bell Library-Texas A&M University-CC

Photos-McGregor Collection-C.C. Museum

(Top) The 'natural beauty' of the Bayfront was not a pretty sight. Below is an excavation preparatory to installing a retaining wall. Below that is an improved Water Street. It was still on the water but not for long. Soon it was just another inland drive.

Photos–C.C. Museum

the Pope to take over the country was reflected in a joke circulated after the election. Smith, the story went, had sent the Pope a one-word telegram: "Unpack."

Fortunately, the 1960 campaign and election of another Catholic, John F. Kennedy, seemed to dispel such fears.

In the local controversy the parties were about equally divided, and both stubbornly refused to compromise. Klansmen planned a march, but anti-Klan deputies manned machine guns atop buildings and the parade was held in Robstown instead.

Tempers flared until blood was shed. One leader was murdered on a public street. Rage con-

(Far left) The Pier Cafe, the white building on the right, is no longer on a pier. It is hemmed in by the rising flow of clay pumped in from the bay floor. The Nueces Hotel lost its status as a seashore attraction.

The dredge boat creates a fountain of mud as thousands of cubic yards of material are pumped in. The newly completed seawall gleams white in the background, and Corpus Christi Cathedral shows up well standing alone on the Bluff.

(Right) The freshly filled addition to the Bayfront has an artificial look. Cheap tourist cabins stand isolated from the beach. The white area at the bottom of the picture would later become the city barge dock.

McGregor Collection-C.C. Museum

tinued until there was a bloody shoot-out, in which hired gunmen on both sides shot each other down at close range. That apparently lanced the boil of hatred. In later years no one on either side would discuss that time when the town turned on itself.

The excesses of that period seemed to have made the citizens more tolerant, and the city has reflected that attitude.

McGregor Collection-C.C. Museum

The city's growth meant, among other things, an increased attention to tourism. Before World War I Victoria had ruled the waves, here as elsewhere.

It seemed that the queen herself had written the rules on beachwear—no bare skin! Women definitely wore bathing suits, not swimsuits. The ladies would have drowned in the outfits, which included skirts well below the knees, stockings and high-top canvas shoes.

For that reason the bath houses were out on piers that had all the comforts of a first-class resort—dance floors, saloons, restaurants, bowling alleys, and a hotel.

Ladies could lower themselves modestly into the water. If they cared to lounge on the beach, they didn't have to worry about sunburn.

When the men returned from World War I, they had seen Paree—and probably wanted to see more of their women.

The one-piece swimsuit was born. Now the girls could actually swim or show off their con-

tours. They could even get their calves sunburned—a landmark in women's lib.

The weather also had something to do with the changing scene on the Bayfront. The 1916 storm washed away all the piers except the Pavilion, and 1919 took care of that one. Piers on the Downtown waterfront would make a comeback, but for fishing and boating, not for bathing.

Harry Corkill, a ship captain, described the fishing.

"With a cane pole you could catch all the trout and redfish you wanted right from the shoreline," he said. "With a cast net you could fill a bucket with big bay shrimp. There were turtles everywhere and you could walk out and gather oysters.

"Dredges scooped the oyster beds clean, killing them. Louisiana and local shrimp trawlers came into the bay and swept it clean of shrimp. Turtles disappeared and the fishing became bad until netting was regulated."

Hundreds of sidewalk engineers kibitz from the steps of the new seawall as the Pleasure Pier becomes the Peoples Street T-Head.

Beaches in front of both the Nueces and Princess Louise Hotels had disappeared by November 1, 1939, as the Bayfront began to take its final form.

McGregor Photo-C.C. Public Library

Workmen install reinforcing steel before pouring concrete.

The contractor, J. DePuy of San Antonio, invented a portable metal form to roll on tracks, which allowed completion of 40 feet of wall each day.

Photos-C.C. Museum

Corkill estimated he had captained 60 boats in his day. The most popular was the *Japonica*, which sported a dance floor and string orchestra. The cruises cost 50 cents, and the boat was the courting area for most of the town's young people of the period.

During Prohibition "the sheriff raided the boat to confiscate 3.2 beer," Corkill said. "He told me I was under arrest. I told him he was under arrest since I was captain of a vessel and therefore a federal officer.

"The headlines said, 'Sheriff, Captain, Arrest One Another.' I started to take him over to Rockport and put him in the brig, but I didn't."

The sheriff considered it a standoff and thought better of the arrest.

The *Japonica* played a major role in another Prohibition tale. In 1933 most of the country was celebrating the repeal of the 18th Amendment with a drink or two. Not so in Texas. Under state law Corpus Christi was still dry territory.

The State Bar was meeting here, and the *Japonica* helped moisten the alcoholic drought just a dram.

It's unconscionable for a gaggle of lawyers to meet without a goodly supply of branch water, so a local delegation was dispatched to Lake Charles, La., where booze and beer were legal, to lay in a supply. Unfortunately, the crew, made up entirely of barristers, felt obligated to splice a few main braces—or whatever they say in seaman talk when they drink toasts to God, Mother, Uncle Sam, and a few passing seagulls.

As a result, the venerable *Japonica*, which had made enough rum runs to operate on the fumes, ran aground, nearly suffered a collision at sea, sur-

Corpus Christi was entering a new era, but don't tell the mules about it. Mulepower was used in a number of the grading and leveling operations.

(Below) The T-Heads await fill.

(Below right) New fill gleams white as snow.

(Opposite) An aerial photo shows cloudiness in the water during dredging. The port was limited to a small turning basin, which would be expanded almost immediately. City streets stand out in sharp relief like a grid because they were paved with white shell, with few trees to mute the glare.

Photos-McGregor Collection-C.C. Museum

McGregor Photo-Caller-Times

One of the first organizations on the new Bayfront was the USO, which provided aid and activities for servicemen. The building became an American Legion Post, the City Tax Office, and then the Art Center of Corpus Christi.

The air was constantly humming with formations of military aircraft during World War II as thousands of pilots, including future President George Bush, trained at Naval Air Station Corpus Christi.

McGregor Collection-C.C. Museum

Art Center of Corpus Christi

vived a sudden storm. It was not surprised to find a Texas Ranger waiting for her at dockside.

The Ranger put the collar on the legal-eagle skipper. All seemed lost until a young lawyer kept the Ranger engaged while the precious cargo was smuggled ashore.

The enterprising lawyer was Price Daniel, later governor, possibly elected because most of the lawyers and judges of the state felt genuinely indebted to him.

Mrs. J.F. McCord, who was Miss Willie Irene

Hatherly when she was queen of the ball at the opening of the new port in 1926, told of another romantic dancing spot famous in local lore.

"My father owned the *Colonel Keith*, a white sailing ship that hauled lumber to my father's companies in Mexico," she said.

"He sold timbers to oil companies in Mexico. We left when Mexico nationalized the American oil companies in 1923.

"It was the first ship to pass under the Bascule Bridge into the new harbor in 1926, towed by

the tug, *Colonel Rockwell*, which was a minesweeper in World War I. This was before the port officially opened.

"The ship was purchased by Bruce Collins, who built the North Beach Amusement Park. He converted it into a floating danceland. It was destroyed in the hurricane of 1933."

The big white vessel was known accurately if not imaginatively as "The Ship."

Despite such attractions, the ambience of the Bayfront left something to be desired. In 1928 the

Gull watching was a top priority for sailors on the newly constructed Bayfront during World War II. Actually, the gobs are watching the girls while the girls are watching the gulls, who are watching for a handout.

McGregor Collection-C.C. Museum

Christmas decorations were up on Peoples Street with the new Robert Driscoll Hotel on the Bluff and the Nueces Hotel on the right. The date— December 5, 1941, two days before the Pearl Harbor attack.

Caller-Times

Chamber of Commerce said the Bayfront "offends the sight and nose."

Thus was the modern Bayfront conceived and born in spite of disappointments and controversy. A local paper dated December 22, 1890, had

In this photo of the skyline, landscaping is in its early stages but still a definite improvement.

(Opposite page) Sailboats frame Corpus Christi Cathedral. Sailing regattas add flair to the seascape nearly every week.

C.C. Public Library

featured a full-page story headlined "A Look into the Future." It predicted a great bayfront improvement. It also predicted, "In 1892 or '93 a keen visioned chap came along and secured the right to build a wall five hundred feet out from the shoreline, filling up back of this wall and utilizing the ground thus acquired. This wall to be built a few feet above the highest wave line for the length of a mile.

"Filling in behind it, he utilized the first 210 feet for a promenade, the next 100 feet for a street and the balance for business."

The writer was off by half a century, but he had the right idea.

Galveston's new seawall had already proved its worth in a 1915 hurricane. In 1915 Corpus Christi

Caller-Times

Steps on the new seawall make a natural grandstand for such activities as watching speedboat races, fireworks displays, and sailboats passing by.

The Bayfront was glaring and shadeless shortly after the war. There were few trees in the city and none on the T-Heads. But fishing was good.

McGregor Collection-C.C. Museum

had tried to get water rights three leagues into the Gulf of Mexico. The Legislature thought the idea too ambitious and the effort failed. But the 1916 storm showed a need for protection; and in 1917 the Legislature passed a bill granting the city ad valorem taxes collected in Nueces, Jim Wells, Jim Hogg, Brooks, Kleberg, Willacy and Duval Counties for 15 years.

The 1919 storm hit before a proposed $500,000 seawall could be built. A 12-foot wall was proposed in 1920, but the project was put off until a channel was dug and a breakwater put in place.

Nothing was done, but the ad valorem tax limit was extended to 25, then 35 years.

A Bay Front Committee from the city administration and the Chamber, set up to maximize "the artistic possibilities of the situation," succeeded in securing the aid of Gutzon Borglum, the

In the 1940s, shortly after its completion, the Bayfront shows a starkness softened by palms, shrubs, plants, and grass.

This aerial view was taken just prior to the construction of Harbor Bridge, before railroads and highways were rerouted.

These photos of a ship leaving the port seem identical until you notice the buildings that have disappeared from the shot (above) taken in 1939, and the other (right) taken in 1965. The Downtown Baptist and First Methodist Churches are gone, as are many fine old residences. The Federal Courthouse and the Caller-Times are visible in both shots, but the row of palm trees in the later one illustrates the development of Shoreline Boulevard.

L.H. Gross Collection-Special Collections & Archives-Bell Library-Texas A&M University-CC

famed sculptor of Mount Rushmore. He submitted a plan which roughly approximates the present seawall: That "a concrete wall be erected approximately 500 feet from the present irregular shoreline. A fill will be pumped in behind this wall and upon the fill a system of parks and boulevards will be placed. . . .

"Midway of its length and immediately opposite the downtown business section the improvement will swing outward in a great central esplanade over 2000 feet long. This esplanade will extend into the water some 400 feet beyond the rest of the work.

"It will form not only the key and pivot for the whole system, but will provide a great seaside coliseum, from which thousands of people can conveniently watch the play of the waves or thrill to the excitement of speed boat races and other aquatic sports . . . ."

His proposal also called for a statue of Christ, which would appear to be walking on water:

"It is the plan to erect in the waters of Corpus Christi Bay a colossal of the Christ. . . It will be bronze and will tower 32 feet above the changing waters of the Bay that bears the name "Body of Christ.'"

Borglum's plan was backed by Mrs. Lorine Jones Spoonts, president of the Chamber. A bond issue was planned, but she returned from a summer trip to learn that the vote had been delayed by the Lovenskiold administration, which then prepared a plan of its own.

The city's plan proposed a seawall only four feet high, with a balustrade like the one on the Bluff around it. The $1.6 million project had no Jesus in it.

Mrs. Spoonts said the plan would create 10 blocks of mud flats, with no room for boats and yachts.

The city engineer wrote of the four-foot seawall, "Any water coming over it will be quickly returned to the bay." The voters didn't swallow that. They killed the plan in a bond election in 1930.

Borglum said Secretary of the Interior Harold Ickes, with whom he had worked getting funds for

Harbor Bridge construction, well under way, was completed in 1959. IH 37 construction can be seen in the foreground.

In this view Harbor Bridge road decking and steel superstructure are nearly in place, dwarfing the Bascule Bridge below.

(Opposite page) The capricious nature of coastal weather may be seen with the boiling tempest stirred up by Hurricane Carla in 1961 and the peaceful shoreline scene below. The seawall did its job and protected the T-Heads from the surging storm tides.

C.C. Public Library

Jack Blackwell Photography

his Mount Rushmore project, had favored helping Corpus Christi. But, he said, representatives from the city descended on Washington and unwittingly killed chances for a federal grant.

In 1934 he wrote of Corpus Christi, "I don't think I have ever seen a town where the crooks and the "respectable" people are so like scrambled eggs."

Some claimed that the sculptor's plan was defeated by other hotel owners who thought the monument would bring too many visitors to the Nueces Hotel, which was owned by Mrs. Spoonts' family. The statue had also met with religious opposition, which undoubtedly helped bring about its defeat.

Borglum and his son, Lincoln, then proposed to erect the statue on Spearfish Mountain in South Dakota, but religious opposition once more defeated them. However, Borglum's idea of a Bayfront development as amphitheater lives on, as the present seawall has been used as a grandstand for fireworks, boat races, and other aquatic events.

When Pope John Paul II visited the United States in 1987, many local residents hoped he would visit the city named "Body of Christ." Inadequate local seating, however, would have been a problem.

One local church official jokingly suggested that the seawall could seat a multitude, and the Pope be towed along the Bayfront on a barge.

Courtesy of Mike Ellis

By the end of the 1930s, oil production and developed farm lands in the seven counties produced enough money to finance construction without requiring Corpus Christi voters to pay off the bonds. The seawall was financed entirely with these state funds.

The new plan was roughly the same as Borglum's except for the T-Heads and L-Head. Original plans called for another L-Head. It was eliminated to cut expenses, but there was enough to pave two broad lanes of Shoreline Boulevard. Construction began in 1939 and was completed in 1941. Myers and Noyes were consulting engineers on the job, and the contractor was J. DePuy of San Antonio.

Hydraulic fill from the bay bottom was a messy goo of clay until it hardened. This caused one young reporter to look for a job elsewhere.

Known for hoaxes, he pulled his last one here when he published a rumor that emplacements

Caller-Times

To a native driving down Shoreline every day things look the same. But pictures taken a few years apart show that the skyline does change as banks, motels, and luxury hotels replace parking lots and older buildings. The photo below was taken in 1971, the one to the right a few years later. It's a mistake to try to tell the years by the size of the palm trees. They are smaller in the later photo because a severe freeze killed the Washatonia palms along the boulevard, and they were replanted.

Photos-C.C. Public Library

were being prepared on the bayfront for 16-inch coastal defense cannon. Leading citizens, councilmen, county commissioners had to check it out. As they walked over the fill, which was crusted on top, they broke through and sank in the muck, ruining suits, shoes and probably a hat or two.

That's when the reporter made a hasty decision to check into job opportunities in Mexico City.

The Bayfront stood starkly bare and glaringly white all during World War II. Nothing would grow on the clay surface. After the war there were many priorities for a fast growing city—streets, sewers, drainage. They didn't include money for park development.

They didn't, that is, until Evelyn Price came along. President of the Garden Club and no shrinking violet, she was named to head the City Parks Department.

When the City Council firmly resisted all efforts to increase the park budget, Mrs. Price enlisted the help of community women. At council meetings the room was packed with determined gardeners and beautifiers.

No council could stand such an onslaught. The funds were found for trees, shrubs, grass, and other greenery. Evelyn Price founded the Civic Beautification Association and continued the campaign.

Clubs and churches were enlisted in the drive, which became a civic movement. Palms and grass gave a barren landscape a definite tropical look. At the same time the *Caller-Times* encouraged an

Caller-Times

The Galvan Band entertains at the bandstand on the Peoples Street T-Head in 1965. The stand and another in Cole Park offer free concerts.

(Bottom left) Shrimp boats seek asylum at the approach of Hurricane Beulah in 1967. The storm brought major flooding.

(Bottom) The pump station shown is one of two, in buildings locals pass and never notice, that lift storm water out of Downtown.

After suffering hurricane damage, the seawall at Cole Park was replaced in a park enlargement, and a landfill created a much larger recreation area.

C.C. Public Library

almost treeless city to plant by selling trees at cost. The new look won Corpus Christi the national Good Housekeeping Beautiful City Award in 1951. Civic pride has kept the Bayfront as Mrs. Price would have wanted it.

Later it was the Organization for the Preservation of an Unblemished Shoreline (OPUS) that clashed with businessmen over the size of signs on the shoreline and types of businesses on Shoreline Boulevard. Armed with city ordinances, OPUS policed the Bayfront. Thus it prevented develop-

Courtesy of Mike Ellis

Bill Walraven

ment of a garish midway advertising tattoo parlors, peep shows, and pawn shops, like those found in many oceanfront cities. In a performance at Del Mar College, comedian-pianist Victor Borge laughingly referred to the town as OPUS Christi.

Across the Bascule Bridge, North Beach flourished until well after World War II, when a new causeway opening access to Padre Island contributed to its decline. Vacationers and locals alike preferred the privacy of the long beach and the higher waves of the Gulf.

The beach had made one remarkable comeback. After the 1933 hurricane washed away the Don Patricio Causeway, North Beach had become the playground of the Gulf Coast, with a carnival, bay swimming, and boating. The amusement park featured a Ferris wheel, roller coaster, a skating rink, games, and midway attractions. The salt water pool, complete with diving board that drew major competitions, was the only swimming facility in the area. A covered grandstand surrounded the cypress wood pool.

When an invasion of jellyfish drove swimmers from the bay waters, they could move into it, but public fresh water pools led to its demise. The amusement park continued a few years longer before it, too, waned.

Construction of Harbor Bridge was the death knell for the beach community. Many North Beach businessmen, as well as some city leaders, favored a tunnel under the ship channel. There were heated hearings between proponents and opponents of the tunnel.

Photos-Jack Blackwell Photography

Bypassed by the Harbor Bridge, Corpus Christi Beach was dying in 1967. Grass grew in the abandoned railroad right-of-way. The name had been changed from North Beach in 1959, after a suggestion by Bruce Collins, the leading businessman on the beach.

(Opposite page, left) Shirley Knetig was one of the beauties whose photos were sent across the country to publicize Buccaneer Days in 1968. The New Year's Day Swim also publicized the tropical nature of South Texas weather, even though it was sometimes freezing.

However, the State Highway Department vetoed the underground route. Since the state was providing funding for the project, the Highway Department had the upper hand, and a high level bridge was built.

Traffic had passed through the beach business district and over a narrow opening spanned by the drawbridge. The "Bascule Bottleneck," as it was called, became a problem for both ship and motor traffic.

Autos backed up for miles when the span was up. Large ships were unable to enter the 90-foot entrance to the harbor, and ships banged into the bridge several times, causing damage that forced motorists to detour around the bay.

Even "Old Ironsides," the *USS Constitution*, nudged the bridge during a 1932 visit and had to have timbers in her hull repaired.

When Harbor Bridge opened in 1959, vehicles whirred overhead bypassing the district completely. Most shops along the strip went out of business.

Earlier the amusement park, worn and shabby, had closed and the Beach Theater abandoned for lack of customers.

This time recovery was slow. Bruce Collins, Sr., owner of the amusement park, swimming pool and other property, had seen the ups and downs on the beach since he started business there in 1919. In 1960 he began the upgrade by building the Sandy Shores Motor Hotel, but it was years

Hurricane Celia, on August 3, 1970, was the most vicious non-surge windstorm ever to hit the Texas coast. The Marina office, its flag in tatters, rides it out.

Collapsing brick walls caused heavy damage in the Downtown area.

Photos-Caller-Times

A resident pauses for refreshment as he surveys his domain—or what's left of it.

Celia victims line up outside Exposition Hall on Shoreline to seek Red Cross disaster aid.

before others would follow suit. Eventually condominiums and other businesses came. But it was not until the Texas State Aquarium opened in 1990 that the beach began to shed its grubby reputation.

Restaurants and new shops appeared. The beach was rejuvenated with river sand to correct a serious erosion problem created by Hurricane Beulah and to provide a wide area for bathers and sun worshipers.

And the arrival of the *Lexington* furnished new inspiration for a full recovery.

Although the new bridge was bad for the beach, it was tremendous for the Port of Corpus Christi and the economy of the city. A channel 200 feet wide and 34 feet deep immediately increased the tonnage of the port. Eventually it became the eighth in the nation.

The story on the south side of the ship channel is similar to that on the north side. The bridge brought something of a depression there, too, except for the attraction of tourists to watch ocean going ships come and go. The main activity took place at the city barge dock, where pipe and supplies were loaded for bay and offshore drilling rigs, which often docked there for outfitting and repairs.

The dock later became a parking lot for the Art Museum of South Texas and Bayfront Convention Center and the rest of the Bayfront complex, the pride of the city.

With the growth of suburban shopping centers and malls, businesses moved out and the Downtown area also suffered a downsurge. Moving the people magnets—City Hall, the Courthouse and the Library—Uptown hurt Downtown, too. But new businesses with different focus grew there.

'Sea Bird,' by Francisco Turegano, stands in front of Harbor Playhouse. It was judged the best in a contest for Bayfront art shortly after the opening of Bayfront Plaza Convention Center.

You'd definitely have had spots before your eyes at the Art Museum of South Texas in 1986 when Jun Keneko displayed 'The Polka Dot Sidewalk.' Each block weighed several hundred pounds.

Bill Walraven

Art Museum of South Texas

The Bayfront, however, experienced no such depression. Tourist, convention and recreational facilities continued to multiply, as hotels, restaurants, banks, and activities on the L- and T-Heads kept the Shoreline vibrant and active.

Walking, jogging, biking, rollerblading, or just sitting continued to make the seawall the greatest people watching spot in town.

Just south of Downtown, Cole Park became another popular people spot, as well as an extension of the philosophy of preservation. The ground under it was eroding and the bluff crumbling when the city reclaimed it from the bay.

Soon it was the scene of kite flying and band concerts. On sunny days KidsPlace, a community playground, draws families to the park. This project, celebrating the 50th anniversary of the Junior League, was built in 1991 in five days by 3,871 volunteers.

Strangely, KidsPlace can trace its origin to the city's long military connections. E.B. Cole had wanted to build a park, preferably one around the North Beach rifle pits of Zachary Taylor's army. No one else thought it was a good idea, so, on April 23, 1939, Cole donated the land he owned to the south for the park on Ocean Drive.

While such beautification projects have drawn both controversy and praise, the primary purpose of the Bayfront has always been storm protection.

In the 1960s, 70s, and 80s, four storms left their mark on the city: Carla in 1961, Beulah in 1967, Celia in 1970, and Allen in 1980.

Carla, a surge storm, did its major damage further up the coast, near Port Lavaca and Matagorda Island, while Beulah, a major wet storm, brought torrential flooding to all of South Texas. Celia, which struck the city on August 3, 1970, did the worst damage to Corpus Christi.

Photos-Harbor Playhouse

The 1996 Harbor Playhouse production of the musical 'Singin' in the Rain' featured Juliane Causey in the role of Lina Lamont.

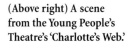

(Above right) A scene from the Young People's Theatre's 'Charlotte's Web.'

(Top) The Veterans Band performs at the Art Museum. The band has taken part in such prestigious events as the 1989 inauguration of President George Bush.

Bill Walraven

Illustrating the area's Hispanic heritage, this statue of Carlos III, King of Spain from 1759 to 1788, was a Bicentennial gift from Spain to Nueces County. It stands in the courthouse lobby.

Photos-C.C. Business Alliance

Bayfest, which originated in 1976 to mark the Bicentennial, became a major fall celebration, drawing thousands of celebrants of all ages. A summer jazz festival also draws crowds to the Downtown area.

Celia was a strange storm, not a typical hurricane. Most lose velocity when they pick up forward momentum, but Celia rapidly accelerated her forward movement, and velocity increased tremendously. Winds in the vortex at times reached an estimated 200 miles an hour. It was like a giant tornado. A rickety shed would remain intact, while a concrete and steel building next door would be ground to a pulp.

Two-by-four timbers came in one wall and went out the other. One woman poured a glass of wine and set the bottle down. A piece of timber came through the kitchen with such force it tore the top of the bottle away without disturbing the contents. Somehow or another a horse ended up in the yard of a house near Annaville. The fence was intact. The horse was uninjured and apparently in good health. Nobody knew where the horse came from, and nobody claimed it. The mystery of the flying horse was never solved.

A few brave boatmen decided to ride out the storm on their boats. They had done it before in other storms, but this was not the one to mess with. Capt. Eddie Mathisen, who had finally managed to own his own boat, the *Renegade*, recalled, "It was supposed to be 75 miles an hour or so. No worse than a spring storm."

He and a friend put out extra mooring lines, took aboard a couple of six-packs, and waited.

"The winds came from the northwest and pushed all the water from the boat basin. We were sitting in the mud. Leon Brown held his beer up in a toast. About that time the charthouse took off, spinning 500 feet in the air.

"My boat rose up in the air, like it was on a wave. It was the wind. It came down on top of a

14-inch piling, which crushed through the hull. Naturally, I didn't have any insurance."

He and Brown crawled across Shoreline Boulevard holding onto the curbs. The storm removed Capt. Eddie from the ranks of the self-employed.

A family in an expensive neighborhood saw their home was beginning to disintegrate. They took shelter in a windowless closet in the middle

Buccaneer Days fireworks light up the spring skies, and the Harbor Lights celebrations brighten up the Bayfront at Christmastime.

George Gongora

Caller-Times

The aerial view shows the havoc Allen played with boats in the marina. Debris cluttered the T-Heads, which had been inundated by several feet of water.

The remains of a home crushed by Allen's waves at the far end of Corpus Christi Beach. A great many houses either were destroyed or had to be condemned after the storm.

Dean Thorpe

of the house. To their horror, water began to rise. Terrified, they watched as the level went from knee deep to waist deep and finally chest deep. They knew they would drown if they stayed there. They decided to face the flood outside and swim for it. When they opened the closet door, all the water ran out. The closet had been flooded by a broken water pipe. It was just as well they had used the closet as a shelter. The house was nearly demolished—all but the closet.

A young agriculture writer left his second-floor apartment when it began to break up. He took shelter in an office on the first floor.

When the winds diminished, he checked his apartment. The entire second floor of the building was gone, along with his clothing, personal belongings, and furniture.

The one exception was the telephone table, with the telephone still on it. He picked it up and got a tone. It was working. He called the operator

Courtesy of Mike Ellis

Caller-Times

Courtesy of Mike Ellis

Hurricane Allen, in August 1980, started out as the hurricane of the century, with a radar persona that covered the entire Gulf of Mexico. Luckily, it stayed off coast long enough to lose some of its punch. Still its tide, the highest since the 1919 storm, caused heavy damage. Corpus Christi Beach was particularly hard hit. The crushed house, submerged car and sunken boat illustrate the damage.

Near the harbor the seawall collapsed. The broken opening view gives a view of the tanker *Mary Ellen*, which ran aground near the channel. The seawall had held up well in the saltwater environment, but engineers warned that the storm-buffeted structure would require major repairs after 50 years.

Caller-Times

George Gongora

During Hurricane Beulah in 1967, several hundred people had taken refuge in the National Guard Armory. It was fortunate they didn't take the same precautions for Celia. Because it was reported as a minimal hurricane, people stayed at home. Meanwhile concrete and brick walls at the armory came tumbling down. Had there been people there, the toll would have been appalling.

Celia did not diminish greatly when it went ashore, but continued with winds nearly 120 miles an hour as far inland as Del Rio. It left in its wake more property damage than any storm in modern Texas history.

Celia was a windstorm, pure and simple, not a giant wet tornado with a surging flood tide. Celia proved something that old time storm watchers have known for years. Every storm is different. The moral is: Never take a hurricane for granted. It probably hasn't read the rule book.

When it comes to the Bayfront, "It's always something." No matter what the project, somebody is against it. For example, the stainless steel twin dolphins in the lobby of what became Nations Bank. They were first proposed as art for the median out front.

There was an immediate howl that the bank's logo was a dolphin, which would make the statue an advertisement. Then, after the sculpture was— in the words of sculptor Kent Ullberg— "anchored to China," the bank's affiliation changed and the dolphin was no longer the logo. Even then, there would have been opposition, for one civic leader said of such art, "I don't want to see any more feathers or fins on the Bayfront."

Much more far-reaching was the controversy over Bayfront Plaza Convention Center.

and said, "I want to discontinue service on my telephone."

"Why?" asked the astonished operator. "Yours is the only working phone in your area. Are you sure you want it disconnected?"

"Yes," he replied. "There's no house around it."

City Manager Marvin Townsend had his own unique filing system. Letters, requests, and other documents were piled high on his desk. He knew where everything was, but nobody else did and projects and requests he considered to be of low priority got lost in the stacks.

After Celia he didn't have to stonewall it. The windows exploded, and all those pending matters went sailing out into Corpus Christi Bay.

But that was the least of his troubles. During the storm Townsend and a reporter jumped out of his city car at the police station. Seconds later the police radio tower came crashing down, smashing his car, crushing it where the two had been sitting.

There's a lot to see on the Bayfront. You can see even better if you feed the field glasses (opposite page) a coin.

(Bottom) You can take the retired ferry now acting as a water taxi. Here it passes by the outdoor bird sanctuary at the Texas State Aquarium. Or, if you're adventurous enough, you might want to take a spin at water ski-ing or take a high speed sightseeing tour on a splinter of a boat.

Or maybe you'd prefer a slower pace (left) on a paddle boat or on a side-walk pedal surrey.

Bill Walraven

C.C. Business Alliance

Photos-George Gongora

C.C. Business Alliance

The Bayfront is for families. KidsPlace in Cole Park is a good place to start.

Then you can get a workout by taking the family for a spin in a surrey (middle right). It's easy to pedal with the wind, but you may have to push coming back against it.

In 1939 Mayor A.C. McCaughan had advocated building an auditorium on "fill now being prepared on the new shoreline," but nothing came of his proposal.

A City Hall, a tax office, an Exposition Hall, and Memorial Coliseum were all built in the early 1950s in the Shoreline Boulevard median. A nearby park was created and named Sherrill Park, in honor of Warren Joseph Sherrill, a Corpus Christi resident killed on the *USS Arizona* during the attack on Pearl Harbor in 1941. By the 1990s, all the buildings except the coliseum were gone.

It had long been obvious that a new convention facility was necessary, Philip Johnson, designer of the Art Museum of South Texas, envisioned a theater, open air dance pavilion, planetarium, aviary and a display of flags of all the nations in the world, but that grand plan was not to be.

It took three elections and court action to overcome heated opposition to a convention complex. The Bayfront Civic Auditorium was approved first. It opened in 1978 with a performance by the U.S. Army Field Band and Soldiers Chorus. After still more controversy and a long court fight, land was acquired for the rest of the complex.

In 1995 the auditorium was renamed the Selena Auditorium, in honor of Tejano music star Selena Quintanilla-Perez. The Corpus Christi resident was murdered on March 31, 1995. Yolanda Saldivar, an employee and founder of her fan club, was convicted and sentenced to life in prison for the shooting.

In 1993 Selena had won a Grammy award for the best Mexican-American performance album, "Selena Live." An especially tragic aspect of her untimely death was the fact that she was preparing to expand into mainstream pop. Although she gained fame in the Tejano music field, English was her primary language. After her death, the *Caller-Times* reported, her posthumous "Dreaming of You" sold five million albums in the first six months after its release. Thousands of fans who loved Selena in life and others who discovered her fame only after her tragic death have come to Corpus Christi to pay homage to her memory.

Another tragedy had given rise to one of the most obvious improvements along the Bayfront, the eight *miradores*, sheltered white concrete octagons, with tile roofs and floors. They offer a place to stop in the shade for a drink of water and learn a bit of local history.

The *miradores*, vantage points Nordic Americans might call gazebos, were financed by the Devary Durrill Foundation, which provided $1 million. The city paid about $100,000 to provide water and electricity at each structure.

Devary Durrill was a 19-year-old killed in

Photos-C.C. Business Alliance

Wilson Walraven

The 'Golf' of Mexico: Buccaneers stalk the beach at the Pirates of the Gulf miniature course.

And adventurous kids will demand a turn at the wheel of a midget racer.

'Friendship Monument,' by Dr. Sherman Coleman, stands on the Bayfront dedicated to the memory of Capt. Blas Maria de la Garza Falcon, the area's earliest settler and rancher. Historians generally credit his family with naming Corpus Christi Bay, from which the city gets its name.

After viewing the exhibits, patrons of the Art Center can lunch at the tea room and look across Shoreline Drive for a fine view of the marina and the Corpus Christi Yacht Club (below).

Art Center of C.C.

Photos-Bill Walraven

1978 when her Ford Mustang II exploded in flames after it was struck from the rear. Proceeds from a multi-million dollar lawsuit the Durrill family won against Ford Motor Co. financed the foundation.

Probably the most controversial of all Bayfront proposals—except for a far-out idea to build a freeway just offshore from Ocean Drive—was Bayfront Associates' Landmass development. It would have been a nine-acre land fill north of the Peoples Street T-Head, with stores not to exceed two stories, shops, and originally an aquarium.

It started out as an idea to draw more tourists to the Bayfront, but ended up as the largest city lawsuit in terms of damages sought—$46 million

in actual and punitive damages. A jury awarded the developers $2.4 million. However the Thirteenth Court of Appeals overturned the verdict in 1991. In 1983 the grand plan called for 150,000 square feet of commercial space and 400 boat slips. The City Council, refusing to call a referendum on the issue, accepted the plan.

A series of angry meetings followed; OPUS, the Taxpayers Association, environmental groups, and others loudly objected. The plan cleared the Federal Emergency Management Agency (FEMA), the Environmental Protection Agency, and the National Fisheries Service.

Each hearing was a mob scene as nasty as any fought over the Bayfront since the Yankees tried to grab it in the Civil War.

Art Center of C.C.

Carroll High School art student Chris Doray fashioned this rendition of Pompeo Coppini's Confederate Memorial with a twist the Italian artist might not have understood. The work, of drawing ink and watercolor, was shown at the Art Center.

Sculptor Pompeo Coppini, who fashioned the Cenotaph at the Alamo and Littlefield Fountain at the University of Texas, was commissioned by the local United Daughters of the Confederacy to create a memorial to Confederate dead. The fountain just below the Bluff was dedicated in 1914. It is supposed to be Corpus, Queen of the Gulf, being crowned by Mother Earth and Neptune, with additional allegorical sidebars.

C.C. Business Alliance

The cultural complex includes the Corpus Christi Museum of Science & History, with the Columbus ships in the outside museum, and, across the way, the USS Lexington Museum and Texas State Aquarium.

(Opposite page bottom) Figures in a museum diorama of life in the Great Market of the ancient Aztec city of Tlatelolco blend skillfully with the painted backdrop to create a three-dimensional effect.

The Buddha and pagoda are among the extensive collection of rare artifacts at the Asian Cultures Museum and Educational Center, located across Chaparral Street from the Museum of Science & History.

Bill Walraven

C.C. Museum

C.C. Business Alliance

Then on February 4, 1986, the Texas State Aquarium Association abandoned plans to build on the landmass. Three weeks later the Corps of Engineers withdrew its permit. FEMA had decided businesses on such an exposed location could not be insured. A scaled down version was offered and eventually it all ended in the lawsuit and the final appeal.

Most of the hue and cry arose because the city would not let the people vote on the issue.

(Middle left) The entrance to the Museum of Science & History has been xeriscaped with attractive native plants that require little precious water.

This model of a 16th century carrack is part of an exhibit that shows the evolution of shipbuilding during the days of Spanish colonization.

Photos-Bill Walraven

Christopher Columbus stands outside the James C. Storm Pavilion at the Port of Corpus Christi.

C.C. Business Alliance

Caller-Times

Still more objections arose when the drive began to "Land the Lex," to bring the retired aircraft carrier *USS Lexington* here as a naval museum.

On August 29, 1990, the Navy announced that the *USS Forrestal* would replace the *Lexington* as the training carrier in the Gulf of Mexico, with home port at Pensacola, Fla. Although opponents would complain that it would cost too much and would obstruct the view of the bay, the C.C. Area Economic Development Council formed a task force to see if the *Lexington* could come to Corpus Christi as a naval aviation museum. The Lady Lex Museum on the Bay Association received the endorsement of the City Council and the Port Commission to proceed.

Other cities seeking to get the ship were Pensacola, Miami, Quincy, Mass.; and Mobile, Ala. A $3 million local bond issue supported the project. The Lex was decommissioned in Pensacola in November 1991, and on January 23, 1992, Secre-

Port of Corpus Christi

Bill Walraven

'El Circo del Mar,' a statue of brown pelicans, was sculpted by H.W. Tatum, Jr., in 1985. Tatum later received the commission to sculpt the statue of Selena for the *Mirador de la Flor,* erected on the Bayfront in 1997.

(Opposite left) The Merriman-Bobys House in Heritage Park, built in 1852 by Walter Merriman, lawyer and land promoter, was used as a Confederate hospital during the Civil War. Other Heritage Park houses include (opposite right) Gugenheim, Sidbury, and Lichtenstein.

(Bottom left) The tall ship *Elyssa* sails under Harbor Bridge. Based in Galveston, *Elyssa* is a fully operational sailing ship of the 1800s.

The dancing waters of the Watergarden are sculpture in motion. The Watergarden is the centerpiece of the Bayfront Arts & Sciences Park.

C.C. Business Alliance

tary of the Navy H. Lawrence Garrett III awarded the ship to the Corpus Christi Area Convention and Visitors Bureau. The next day the ship began her journey to become a permanent Texan.

Formally designated CV 16 in Navy terminology, the *USS Lexington* is more than a museum. It is a living memorial to all the men who died aboard her, both in combat and in aerial accidents. The Lex herself is a memorial to the previous *Lexington*, CV 2, sunk during World War II in the Battle of Coral Sea, May 8, 1942, and to the Navy's previous warships of the same name.

The Navy's first *Lexington*, named for the opening battle of the American Revolution, fought

Playful otters are the stars of the Texas State Aquarium as they gracefully swim and cavort in their outdoor home on the ground floor.

Texas State Aquarium

Wilson Walraven

in that war. Her 110-man crew took many prizes before British cannon fire destroyed her rigging and she was captured in 1777. The second *Lexington* was a sloop of war commissioned in 1826. She served in the Mexican War and carried Commodore Matthew Perry to Japan in 1853 in that famous visit that opened the door of Japanese trade to the world.

The third *Lexington* was a sidewheeler steamboat commissioned in 1860. It supported Gen. U.S. Grant's Army along the Mississippi River.

The Navy's first aircraft carrier was the *USS Langley*, sunk in 1942 in the Battle of Java Sea. CV 2 was designed as a battle cruiser and originally designated the *Constitution* but was converted to an aircraft carrier named *USS Lexington* December 10, 1917. She was launched October 2, 1925. Her sister ship was the *USS Saratoga*, CV 3. Fleet sailors always referred affectionately to the two carriers as a single entity—the *Lex* and the *Sara*.

It was fortunate that these two grand old sisters were on their way to Pearl Harbor on December 7, 1941, not at anchor there. Had they been destroyed in the Japanese attack, the road to victory would have been much rougher.

In Corpus Christi the *Lex* and *Sara* were honored by the names of the two military highways connecting the Navy's airbases—Lexington and Saratoga Boulevards. Something was lost when Lexington Boulevard was changed to SPID.

Photos-Bill Walraven

Among sculptures on the bay side overlooking the aquarium's wild bird sanctuary and near the turtle exhibit is (middle left) 'Kemp's Ridley Turtles' by Tom Tischler. 'Spring Plumage,' the bronze of a great blue heron, is by Kent Ullberg.

Complete with a bulletin board posting Port of Corpus Christi arrivals and departures, the observation deck on the aquarium's second floor is prime ship-watching territory.

An exterior shot shows the aquarium on its perch at the edge of the ship channel.

A number of seabirds, most of them disabled, and a tank of varied sea life greet visitors at the entrance to aquarium exhibits.

(Opposite page) If you've ever had a strong urge to pet a shark, you can realize your ambition at the shark petting pool. As a bonus, you can stroke a passing sting ray. You won't be bitten or stung, and you'll have quite a story to tell your neighbors.

Texas State Aquarium

The *Saratoga*, though severely wounded in the campaigns of 1945, survived the war but ended up as a melted wreck at the bottom of a lagoon near Bikini Atoll, where it and other warships were destroyed in an atom bomb test in July 1946.

The *Lexington*, mortally wounded by several torpedoes and bombs while trying to blunt an attack by the entire Japanese carrier fleet, was finally dispatched by U.S. destroyers. She lost 26 officers and 190 enlisted men out of a crew of 2,951.

In the spring of 1942 the *USS Cabot*, CV 16, was under construction at Bethlehem Shipyard in Quincy, Mass., when news of the *Lexington*'s sinking was received. Thousands of workers, many of whom had helped build the CV 2, asked that CV 16 also be named *Lexington*. The secretary of the Navy immediately granted the request.

She joined the fleet August 9, 1943, and began her illustrious combat career. Two months later she was providing air cover for Marine landings in

Tugs nudge the 'Blue Ghost,' CV 16, into her final berth alongside the breakwater on Corpus Christi Beach on June 17, 1992, as the USS Lexington Museum.

(Opposite page) Planes resting on her flight deck are not fighting machines but historical artifacts to educate new generations about a great tradition.

(Far right) The mast bristles with radar and communications antennas.

(Bottom right) The battle ribbons reflect a proud tradition. Her Presidential Unit Citation reads: 'For extraordinary heroism in action against enemy Japanese forces in the air, ashore, and afloat in the Pacific War Area from September 18, 1943, to August 15, 1945.'

George Gongora

Jim Cruz/Galveston-Courtesy of USS Lexington Museum

Photos-Hugh Power/Galveston-
Courtesy of USS Lexington Museum

the Gilbert Islands, then a raid on Wake Island. Her tour included Kwajalein. She was struck by a Japanese torpedo on December 4, but managed to make it back to Pearl Harbor. Other campaigns included the Marshall Islands in April 1944. In June she was giving fighter support in the Marianas, an action in which more than 400 Japanese planes were destroyed.

One of her pilots said it was like "shooting turkeys," a statement that gave the Battle of the Philippine Sea its informal designation as the "Marianas Turkey Shoot." In that action a Japanese carrier was sunk and three others damaged.

The Lex seemed to live a charmed life. At least that was the opinion of Tokyo Rose, the propaganda voice of Radio Tokyo, for she reported the *Lexington* sunk in battle after battle. The ship helped secure the Bonins; Mindanao, Cebu-Leyte, and Luzon in the Philippines; and Ulithi.

Exasperated at the Lex's continuing reappearance, Tokyo Rose dubbed her the "Blue Ghost" because of her Measure II Sea Blue paint. The

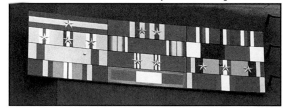

Lexington's wartime ribbons and awards: Gilbert Islands, Marshall Islands, Hollandia, Asia-Pacific Raids, Marianas, Western Caroline Islands, Leyte, Luzon, Iwo Jima, Third Fleet Operations Against Japan, Navy Occupation Service Medal, Philippine Republic, Presidential Unit Citation Badge.

From catching it to putting it on the table, fresh seafood is the name of the game in Corpus Christi, as shown by trawler nets in the boat basin and (right) the shrimp fleet in port.

Landry's (below) is a floating seafood restaurant on the Peoples Street T-Head.

The Lighthouse restaurant (opposite) receives a new lookout in its 1997 expansion. The Lighthouse was also a gift of the wind, as it received a lease after Hurricane Allen destroyed the marina office on the L-Head and the city lacked funds to rebuild.

Photos-Bill Walraven

C.C. Business Alliance

Bill Walraven

crew quickly adopted the name. Her predecessor had been called the "Lady Lex," and the two nicknames would be confused for years.

On December 4, 1943, an aerial torpedo struck the *Lexington's* starboard side, killing nine men and injuring 35. On November 5, 1944, a kamikaze Zero hit the ship's island, killing 47 men and injuring 127. After the kamikaze attack, Tokyo Rose was convinced that the venerable flattop had been scratched, but by the New Year she was back on her battle station in actions around the Japanese home islands. After the surrender she was the first carrier to enter Tokyo Bay.

She was deactivated in May 1946, but overhauled as Korean troubles worsened and recom-

Bayfront attractions include *Miradores*, shady spots to learn a little local history from bronze plaques inside, and an Army helicopter, (opposite page) announcing that the world's largest copter repair facility is here at the Corpus Christi Army Depot.

(Opposite page) Two works by world renowned sculptor Kent Ullberg, NA, grace the Downtown Bayfront area. At left is 'Watermusic,' as performed by three porpoises in polished stainless steel. It is located in the lobby of Nations Bank on Water Street. At right is 'Wind in the Sails,' which was named the top sculpture in America in 1983. It was commissioned by *The Corpus Christi Caller-Times* to commemorate the newspaper's centennial that year.

Bill Walraven

Bill Walraven

Juan Bosquez, C.C. Parks & Recreation Department

C.C. Art Connection

C.C. Business Alliance

missioned in August 1955. After several years of duty with the Pacific Fleet and a stint off Cuba during the missile crisis there, she became the training carrier stationed at Pensacola.

Advanced students from NAS qualified for their carrier landings on her decks. She trained 1,500 pilots a year from 1963 until her 1991 retirement.

A walking tour of the T-Heads gives drylanders as big a treat as the city offers, with a chance to view both working shrimpers and a variety of pleasure craft.

Corpus Christi's Tejano music star Selena was largely unknown to Anglo-Americans before her tragic death in 1995, but she was idolized by millions of Hispanics around the world.

After the City Council gave approval to her permanent site on Corpus Christi Beach, President George Bush signed documents transferring the *USS Lexington* from the Navy to the City of Corpus Christi. She was towed into place June 17, 1992, and opened to the public on October 14, 1992. On November 14 the "Blue Ghost" was formally dedicated.

No one cared to remember that the local delegation had originally called itself the Lady Lexington Association. The old CV 2 probably wouldn't have minded the slip-up.

George Gongora-Caller-Times Photo

Photos-Bill Walraven

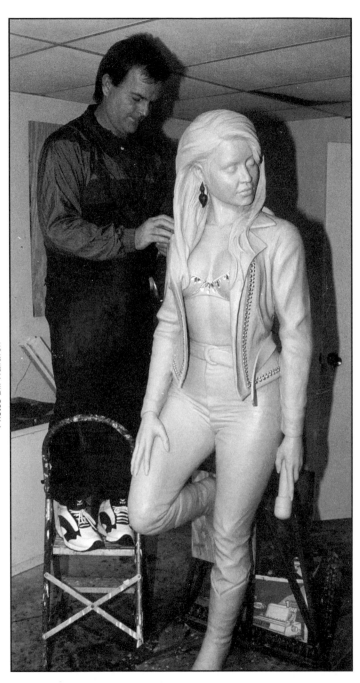

C.C. Business Alliance

A bronze bell in the Museum of Science & History stands as another artifact of World War II.

Surprisingly, it dates back to 1873, for it was the bell of the Corpus Christi Volunteer Fire Department. The bell tolled from a tower atop Market Hall below the Bluff. When fire was reported, it rang out the number of one of four fire districts so volunteer firemen would know which direction to take. Those living far out in the country could hear the bell when it tolled.

The fire chief rang the bell every hour on the hour, and there was a special ring at 9 a.m. on school days. The bell was toppled from its perch during the 1919 storm and placed in a cradle on street level outside the fire department.

At the outbreak of World War II, fire officials volunteered the bell for scrap. However, after the *USS Houston* was sunk in the Battle of Sunda

George Gongora

The Bayfront Plaza Convention Center has been a magnet in attracting top flight meetings to the city. Here city officials from various sections of the state chat between sessions while a bay shrimp trawler passes by. The exhibition hall and meeting facilities, together with a huge increase in the number of hotel rooms available, have kept the convention/tourist business one of the city's leading industries.

(Opposite) The Bayfront auditorium, shown during a symphony performance, was named the Selena Auditorium in memory of the young Tejano singer. She was also honored with her statue on Shoreline Drive in the *Mirador de la Flor*—the vista of the flower—in honor of her love for white roses. (Middle) Sculptor H.W. Tatum, Jr., puts the finishing touches on his model.

(Center) Ships that pass in the day: Tankers entering and leaving the port offer an unusual portrait of modern-day Corpus Christi.

The English were recognized for their seamanship in the days of sail, for they had faster and more efficient men-of-war. But the Spaniards led the way. No other sailors could surpass them in courage. They sailed thousands of miles in fragile vessels designed for fishing and coastwise shipping, crossing vast oceans to places never before seen by Europeans. Many never returned home, but they left their imprint on two continents. The Columbus Fleet ships are memorials to those brave men.

C.C. Business Alliance

Another project, one that did not draw heated opposition, was the Gateway Project to provide a scenic entry from Interstate 37 to the Bayfront. In 1986 there was a plan to install a fountain in the median of the interstate, but the $5 million Gateway project was much more ambitious. It involved shifting the entrance 200 feet westward and replacing several parking lots to make way for a tree-studded six-acre green belt stretching from the old 1914 courthouse to the bay.

The lanes of Shoreline were moved together and the grassy area moved next to the bay, creating a promenade for benches and works of art.

Strait, the bell was sent to the new *Houston*. The crew said the bell had a far better sound than the regulation ship's bell. It's said that since silver was so cheap at the time the bell was cast, it contains a fair amount of that metal, accounting for its melodious tone.

After the *Houston* was decommissioned, the bell was placed in storage until it was volunteered as a war relic for the Battleship Texas Museum at the San Jacinto Battlefield in Houston. It stayed there until local officials asked that the historic old bell be returned to Corpus Christi. Battleship Texas officials agreed—if the regular *Houston* bell would replace it. This was done.

A trolley approaches a popular stop at the Water Street complex, home of the Water Street Oyster Bar and Water Street Seafood Company. Running from hotels to restaurants and convention facilities, trolleys offer one of the better ways of seeing the Bayfront.

To young and old alike, ships are a fascination and a pleasure to watch.

Bill Walraven

Port of Corpus Christi

George Gongora

The centerpiece of this beautification was a new Federal Courts Building. Citizens found the financing less objectionable because of state and federal grants and private contributions.

'The Good Shepherd' at the Episcopal Church of the same name is the work of Dr. Sherman Coleman.

Viewed from above, the Peoples Street T-Head forms a cross, an altogether fitting symbol for a city bearing the name 'Body of Christ.'

Photos-Bill Walraven

Dr. Sherman Coleman collaborated with his daughter, Kathleen Edwards, on the statue of Christ at Spohn Hospital on Ocean Drive. The statue was originally intended to go on public property on the Bayfront.

'Peace,' by Nassan Gobran, is outside Spohn's James R. Daugherty School of Nursing.

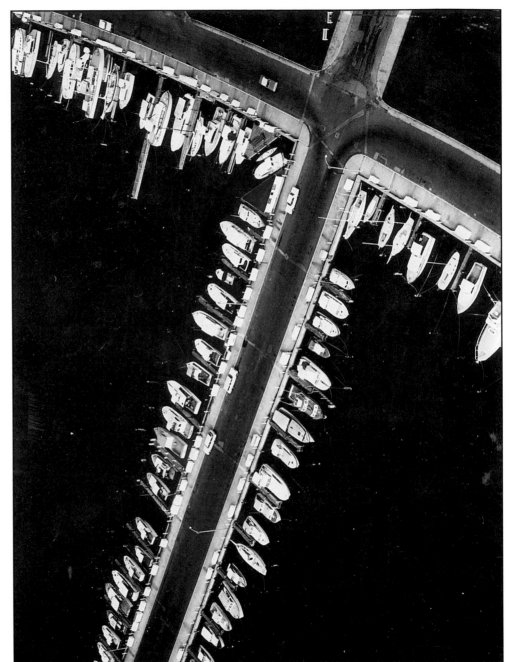

Caller-Times

Phase II of the project was to include a boardwalk and parkway from the Gateway to the Peoples Street T-Head. Thus the Bayfront continued its role as the center of the city's prosperity.

The focus was on the Bayfront Arts & Science Park, with its Museum of Science & History, Art Museum of South Texas, Bayfront Plaza Convention Center, Harbor Playhouse, all surrounding the centerpiece Watergarden.

Corpus Christi Art Connection

These attractions, combined with the Texas State Aquarium; the USS Lexington Museum; The Place, a bilingual theater; and the Corpus Christi International Seaman's Center to form an entertainment and educational complex that drew national attention.

The Spanish shipwreck artifacts, the Columbus Fleet, and the Seeds of Change display combined to make the museum one of the most desirable attractions in Texas.

The Seeds of Change, created by the Smithsonian Institution in 1992, drew more than 10 million visitors before it was donated to the local museum. Showing the impact of disease, horses, and even corn, potatoes, and sugar, it traces the changes that resulted from contact between the ancient cultures of the Western and Eastern Hemispheres.

The Columbus ships were built by the government of Spain to mark the 500th anniversary of the voyages of Christopher Columbus. Millions of people around the world saw them before Spain agreed to let Las Carabelas Columbus Fleet Association make Corpus Christi their permanent home.

Facilities for the ships next to the museum allow visitors to see how seamen lived, and workshops demonstrate their skills. The Nina is a working laboratory and classroom of ancient techniques of seamanship.

Sailing on Corpus Christi Bay, she completes the package of history—de Pineda's voyage, smugglers rowing ashore with their contraband, General Taylor stuck in a mudbank, puny dredges trying futilely to open a passage to the port, Yankee gunboats bombarding the settlement.

Then a great storm, a new harbor, merchantmen, tankers, an aircraft carrier, a nuclear submarine—The Nina reminds us where we started and how far we have come.

No doubt Capt. Henry, first to land with Taylor's army, would find many adherents to his saying that the land of the bayshore really isn't God's chosen land. But most will agree with his assessment—it really is beautiful!

Photo by Margaret Ramage

(Left) The Rev. Mark Allen Doty of the First United Methodist Church congratulates Kent Ullberg as his statue of Christ, 'It Is I,' is dedicated on the lawn of the First United Methodist Church.

Before the dedication the wind prematurely unveils Him. It is fitting that the Prince of Peace stands ecumenically on the Bayfront, bringing His blessing to the city that bears His name.

Index

George Gongora

Bill Walraven

Caller-Times

As long as they aren't looking for snow, people who like a variety of weather will find Corpus Christi the right place. They'll find fog that makes the Lexington resemble a submarine or wind that whips waves into a froth; but most of the time bright sunny weather that shows the beautiful, sparkling face of the city on the Bay.

George Gongora

The end of a perfect day.

Acknowledgments

A book like this is possible only if a lot of people help. There are a limited number of historic photographs. Many publications have used them, and rarely do you encounter some not generally seen.

The hurricane that is the heart of this story did much to destroy records, both written and photographic. Valuable newspaper collections, as well as photographs and negatives, were lost in the flood waters.

This book, like the other two pictorial histories we have written, would have been severely limited without the work of the late John Frederick "Doc" McGregor, who chronicled a good slice of local history. It was our good fortune to have known "Doc" for many years. He was a gentle, generous soul and a competent chiropractor, but he will always be remembered most for his photographs of the people and scenes of the city he loved.

The McGregor Collection at the Corpus Christi Museum of Science & History is an extremely valuable resource. His work is also collected by the Corpus Christi Public Library, the Nueces County Historical Society, Texas A&M University-Corpus Christi, and area libraries.

Many of the scenes of the period from 1868 to 1898 were taken by Louis de Planque, though the credit usually goes to the archive where they may be found.

Special appreciation goes to Bill and Cathy Harrison, who devised this project and whose enthusiasm and support have made it possible.

Thanks to Patricia Murphy at Corpus Christi Museum; Margaret Rose, archivist at the Public Library; Margaret Neu, *Caller-Times* librarian; Esmeralda "Lala" Salazar of Del Mar College, and Dr. Thomas Kreneck, archivist at Texas A&M-CC, and to their organizations.

Thanks also to the USS Lexington Museum, the Art Museum of South Texas, the Texas State Aquarium, the Asian Cultures Museum, the City Parks and Recreation Department, and the Corpus Christi Business Alliance. All were most helpful.

We also thank Dean Thorpe and Darrell Keach for technical assistance and Wendy Keach, Dorothy Kucera, and Doris Waldhelm for reading and pointing out innumerable errors on our proofs.

Finally, special thanks to a very talented and professional photographer, George Gongora, and to Jorge Ruiz of Colourprep, Inc., of Dallas, our prepress expert and guide into the new world of digital production.

This year, for the first time, we did not have the advice and guidance of the late Dan Kilgore, friend and top authority on the history of Corpus Christi. We miss him sorely.

Bill & Marjorie Walraven